loving church

1 CORINTHIANS 10 – 16

by Mark Dever and Carl Laferton

thegoodbook
COMPANY

loving church
the good book guide to 1 Corinthians 10 – 16
This US co-edition published with 9Marks 2013
© Mark Dever/The Good Book Company, 2013.

To learn more about 9Marks and order
more material, visit www.9Marks.org

9Marks
Building Healthy Churches

The Good Book Company
Tel: (US): 866 244 2165
Tel (UK): 0345-225-0880
Tel (int): + (44) 208-942-0880

Email: admin@thegoodbook.co.uk

Websites
N America: www.thegoodbook.com
UK: www.thegoodbook.co.uk
Australia: www.thegoodbook.com.au
New Zealand: www.thegoodbook.co.nz

thegoodbook
COMPANY

ISBN: 9781908317964

Printed in the USA

CONTENTS

introduction: good book guides

Every Bible-study group is different—yours may take place in a church building, in a home or in a cafe, on a train, over a leisurely mid-morning coffee or squashed into a 30-minute lunch break. Your group may include new Christians, mature Christians, non-Christians, moms and tots, students, businessmen or teens. That's why we've designed these *Good Book Guides* to be flexible for use in many different situations.

Our aim in each session is to uncover the meaning of a passage, and see how it fits into the "big picture" of the Bible. But that can never be the end. We also need to appropriately apply what we have discovered to our lives. Let's take a look at what is included:

⊕ **Talkabout:** Most groups need to "break the ice" at the beginning of a session, and here's the question that will do that. It's designed to get people talking around a subject that will be covered in the course of the Bible study.

⊕ **Investigate:** The Bible text for each session is broken up into manageable chunks, with questions that aim to help you understand what the passage is about. **The Leader's Guide** contains **guidance on questions**, and sometimes ☑ additional "follow-up" questions.

⊕ **Explore more (optional):** These questions will help you connect what you have learned to other parts of the Bible, so you can begin to fit it all together like a jig-saw; or occasionally look at a part of the passage that's not dealt with in detail in the main study.

⊕ **Apply:** As you go through a Bible study, you'll keep coming across **apply** sections. These are questions to get the group discussing what the Bible teaching means in practice for you and your church. ⊡ **Getting personal** is an opportunity for you to think, plan and pray about the changes that you personally may need to make as a result of what you have learned.

⊕ **Pray:** We want to encourage prayer that is rooted in God's word—in line with His concerns, purposes and promises. So each session ends with an opportunity to review the truths and challenges highlighted by the Bible study, and turn them into prayers of request and thanksgiving.

The **Leader's Guide** and introduction provide historical background information, explanations of the Bible texts for each session, ideas for **optional extra** activities, and guidance on how best to help people uncover the truths of God's word.

why study 1 Corinthians 10-16?

What can turn a struggling church around? What should we do when a church is compromised by selling out to the culture; or is riven by factional strife; or is dominated by me-first materialism; or is being undermined by uncertainty about the gospel itself? What should we do when we see glimpses of these things in our own lives?

"Be on your guard", wrote one church planter and pastor to one of the most messed-up churches we could imagine. "Stand firm in the faith; be men of courage; be strong.

"Do everything in love."

So wrote the apostle Paul to the first-century Corinthian church (1 Corinthians 16 v 13-14). This was a congregation which seemed to have lost its way. People were disparaging marriage; denying the resurrection; dividing into factions. Its members were using their worldly wealth, leadership positions and God-given abilities to win praise and honor for themselves.

Paul did not give up on them. He did not grow angry with them. He did not lecture them about wasting his time and ignoring his teaching.

He encouraged them to *love their church*. And, in the second half of his first letter to them, he showed them *how* to love their church.

Christian love is no abstract theory. It is not a disembodied, unengaged cheerfulness. Christian love calls us not to desert but to stand guard, not to give up but to stand firm, not to avoid conflict in cowardice but to defend truth in courage. Christian love is Christ-like love.

This was the love that could turn the Corinthian church around and make it the church its members and its city needed it to be. And this is the love that all our local churches need. If we're to be part of a church that encourages its members; that engages with our culture; and that equips us to hold out the gospel—then we need to be a *loving* church.

These eight studies in 1 Corinthians 10 – 16 will enable, motivate and challenge you to love your church. They will show you how, as individuals and as a church, you can "do everything in love". They will show you how to love as Christ did.

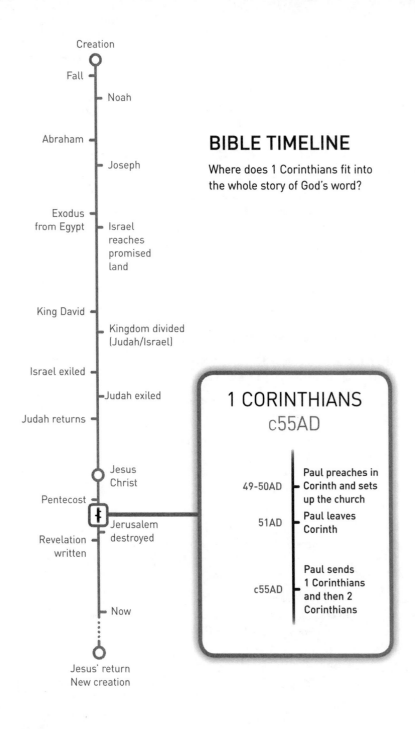

BIBLE TIMELINE

Where does 1 Corinthians fit into the whole story of God's word?

Creation
Fall
Noah
Abraham
Joseph
Exodus from Egypt
Israel reaches promised land
King David
Kingdom divided (Judah/Israel)
Israel exiled
Judah exiled
Judah returns
Jesus Christ
Pentecost
Jerusalem destroyed
Revelation written
Now
Jesus' return
New creation

1 CORINTHIANS
c55AD

49-50AD — Paul preaches in Corinth and sets up the church

51AD — Paul leaves Corinth

c55AD — Paul sends 1 Corinthians and then 2 Corinthians

1

1 Corinthians 9 v 24 – 10 v 13

KEEP ON RUNNING

⊕ talkabout

1. Imagine the starting line of a popular marathon. The starter's pistol goes, and the runners set off. Which of them are really marathon runners?

⊕ investigate

❯ Read 1 Corinthians 9 v 24 – 10 v 4

Paul encourages these church members in Corinth to "run in such a way as to get the prize" (9 v 24)—"a crown that will last forever" (v 25). This is why he is writing to them. He wants these Christians to keep running in faith and obedience, so that they'll make it to the finish line. And to underline his point, he points to an example in history.

> **DICTIONARY**
>
> **Forefathers (10 v 1):** in this context, the spiritual ancestors of Christians—ie: God's people in the Old Testament.
> **Under the cloud (v 1):** When God's people were in the desert, God was present as a cloud, leading them (see Exodus 13 v 21).
> **Baptized into Moses (v 2):** followed and trusted Moses as leader.

2. What period is he focusing on (10 v 1-4)?

• What advantages did these people have?

How do these passages help us appreciate how blessed these people were?

❯ **Read 1 Corinthians 10 v 5-13**

DICTIONARY

3. What is the shock in verse 5?

Idolaters (v 7): people who love and serve a fake god (an idol).
Temptation (v 13): a devil-prompted desire to disobey God.

• Why did this happen?

How do these passages help us appreciate the seriousness of the people's disobedience?

What would these sins look like if they happened in your fellowship?

4. What does 1 Corinthians 10 v 1-10 tell us about God?

• And about following Him?

⊖ apply

5. Why did Paul include these verses in his letter (v 6, 11)?

6. In what ways do we excuse giving into temptation? How does verse 13 both encourage and challenge us?

⊡ getting personal

We can be confident that God will enable us to resist any and every temptation. We face the same temptations as everyone else; and we can outlast all of them, with God's help.

How are you being tempted to disobey God at the moment? When you give in, what excuses do you use? What truth do you need to remember to combat that excuse?

⊡ investigate

These Corinthians had started the Christian race—but the starting line and the finish line are not the same thing. In the first half of the letter, Paul outlined a series of ways in which they were being tempted to disobey God.

7. In pairs or on your own, pick out one or more of the areas in which this church was facing, or giving into, temptation:

- 1 v 11-12:

- 3 v 3:

- 4 v 18:

- 5 v 1-2:

- 6 v 6-7:

- 8 v 8-13:

8. **Read 4 v 10.** How does Paul describe this church's view of him, and of themselves?

- How does this match what you saw in Question Seven?

9. Why did this church need to hear verse 12?

• Why did they need to hear the warning of what happened to the Israelites in Moses' day?

apply

10. Why is complacency—unthinkingly assuming "you are standing firm"—such a danger to a church?

11. When it comes to obeying God, what are the greatest challenges your own fellowship faces?

⊡ **getting personal**

Churches cannot coast along in spiritual things. Regardless of what amazing things we might have seen God do in our congregation, we must continue to rely on Him daily.

Do you pray for your church to grow in godliness as well as in numbers?

Do you encourage other Christians not to be complacent and to keep challenging themselves?

Are there ways in which you need to be careful that you keep on running, and don't fall by the wayside?

⊡ pray

Thank God...

- that He lovingly warns His people.

- that He can see through complacency and hypocrisy.

- that He enables you to resist temptation so that you are able to obey Him.

Ask God...

- to help you to enjoy your blessings, but not to become complacent about your Christian life.

- to help you stand up to temptation (you might like to name a couple of areas in which you are struggling to do this at the moment).

2

1 Corinthians 10 v 14 – 11 v 1

LOVE, LIBERTY AND LEGALISM

The story so far

Paul encouraged the Corinthians to keep running the Christian life by obeying God, and not become complacent about their sin and so risk facing His anger.

⊕ talkabout

1. What expectations can Christians lay on each other which are not found in the Bible? Why do you think Christians do this?

- What issues that the Bible is clear on can Christians often ignore? Why do you think Christians do this?

⬇ investigate

▶ **Read 1 Corinthians 10 v 14-22**

2. What is Paul's clear command in verse 14?

DICTIONARY

Cup of thanksgiving (v 16): a reference to the cup of wine shared at the Lord's Supper (Communion).
Partake of (v 17): take from, share.
Pagans (v 20): people who don't worship the true God.

3. What does he say we are doing when we share the Lord's Supper?

• A lot of Corinthian social and political life had to do with great public feasts held at pagan temples, where the food had been offered to false gods. What does Paul say is really happening at these feasts (v 19-20)?

4. What choice do Christians have to make (v 21)?

⊡ **explore more**

optional
In verses 18-22, Paul is again looking back to the history of Israel, just as he did in 10 v 1-13 (see previous session).

> Read Deuteronomy 32 v 10-22

What had God done for "him" ie: Israel (v 10-14)?

What did Jeshurun (a term for Israel) do in response (v 15-18)?

How do verses 16-17 link with our 1 Corinthians passage?

What was God's response?

How is this a warning both to the Corinthian Christians, and to us, when it comes to idolatry?

⊖ **apply**

An idol is anything someone treats as their god, serving it because they trust it will give them what they need.

5. What are the most-worshiped idols in your culture? Why are they attractive?

6. How might a Christian in your church end up trying to worship *both* God *and* one of these idols? How does this part of 1 Corinthians warn them?

⊡ getting personal

What false gods are you tempted by? What do you talk about most? What interests you most? What excites you most?

What you answer is a good indication of what you worship. Can you work out why these things are particularly attractive to you?

What do you need to do to "flee from idolatry" when it comes to these false gods?

⊕ investigate

▶ **Read 1 Corinthians 10 v 23 – 11 v 1**

The Corinthian Christians said they were free to eat any meat, even though it had been offered to idols before being sold in the markets of the city.

7. What does Paul say about that, and why (v 25-26, 30)?

> **DICTIONARY**
>
> **Permissible (v 23):** allowable, free to do.
> **Beneficial (v 23):** good for you.
> **Questions of conscience (v 25):** asking: "Is this right or wrong?"
> **Greeks (v 32):** a way of saying: "Anyone who isn't Jewish".

8. But it isn't *always* fine to eat meat that's been sacrificed! When wouldn't it be (v 28-29a)?

• Why not?! If someone who worships idols sees Christians eating meat that's been sacrificed to idols, what might they think about Christianity?

Paul is refusing to be *legalistic*. That is, he refuses to forbid what the Bible allows. Even though some people are "denouncing" him for it (v 30), he won't make a rule that eating meat sacrificed to idols is always wrong. But equally, Paul is refusing to say that doing what is "permissible" is always best (v 23). *Liberty* is not his highest priority, so he won't say that eating such meat is always fine.

9. So, if it's not following a rule or enjoying freedom, what should direct a Christian's actions (v 31-32)?

10. Whose good is Paul seeking? What is his primary aim for them (v 33)?

• In 11 v 1, Paul says he's following "the example of Christ". **Read Luke 19 v 1-10.** What does Paul mean?

⊡ apply

11. How is acting legalistically different from acting out of love?

• Is it possible to end up making an idol out of keeping religious rules? How?

12. Think of some real-life circumstances where acting out of love for others means giving up your Christian liberty.

• How could we end up being legalistic in those situations?

⊡ getting personal

Jesus is our great example of loving God and loving others—not prizing his own liberty, nor being legalistic. And Paul tells us to follow those who follow Christ's example.

What kind of examples do you see around you? Do you follow those who lead you toward Christ, rather than away from Him? Whose Christlike example could you seek to copy more?

And what about your own example: are you a good model for others to follow? How are you showing, and how are you not showing, those around you what Christ is like?

⬆ pray

Thank God that Christ Jesus came to "seek and to save what was lost". Thank Him for freeing you from pursuing empty idols or religious rule-keeping; thank Him for making you a part of His people.

If you are happy to, share with the group one or two idols you are each struggling not to worship. Then pray for each other—**ask God** to enable you to worship Him, bring Him glory, and point others to the truth about Him.

3 1 Corinthians 11 v 2-16
LOVING AUTHORITY

The story so far

Paul encouraged the Corinthians to keep running the Christian life by obeying God, and not to be complacent about their sin and so risk facing His anger.

Paul warned the church not to use their freedom to love idols, and not to make rules to avoid idols, but simply to love others as Christ loved them.

⊕ talkabout

1. When is "authority" a good thing? When is it bad?

- What gives one person the right to have authority over another?

⊕ investigate

This is a famously difficult passage! The key theme throughout is that Paul wants to show the inadequacy of autonomy—literally, self-law—as the way to follow Christ. He wants instead to encourage us to welcome and live within the authority God has designed people to live within, in the church and in marriage.

▶ **Read 1 Corinthians 11 v 2-16**

> DICTIONARY
>
> **Head (v 3-7):** Paul sometimes means your actual head (eg: v 4); and sometimes means "person in authority over", as in "headteacher" (eg: v 3).
> **Contentious (v 16):** argumentative.
> **Practice (v 16):** way of doing things.

It helps to remember that the words "men" and "women" in this passage (eg: v 3) also meant "husband" and "wife". I think that these verses were written with husbands and wives uppermost in Paul's mind.

2. What is the relationship between wife and husband (v 3)? Which other relationship does this reflect?

The most wealthy and respected men would pull over their heads a portion of their best toga when leading prayer in the pagan temples, as a way of indicating their high social status.

3. Why would a man doing this in church be dishonoring his "head" (v 3-4)?

• What were men using their roles in the church service to do?

In those days, headgear and hairstyle reflected a woman's marital status. Covered hair showed you were married.

4. How does this help us understand why Paul says what he does in v 5-6?

• What were women (especially married ones) using their roles in church services to do?

⊖ apply

Men do not seek to show how important they are in the 21st-century by covering their heads. And women do not seek to show they are attractive and potentially available by uncovering theirs.

5. What would a church where these things were happening today look like?

6. What would be the impact of both these attitudes and behaviors on a church fellowship?

⊕ investigate

7. Read **Genesis 2 v 18-25**. In 1 Corinthians 11 v 8-10, Paul is looking back to the story of creation. Why is it helpful to be reminded of how things were in the Garden of Eden, before sin entered the world?

• Why is the man the head of a marriage (1 Corinthians 11 v 8-9)?

• Why did God make woman (Genesis 2 v 18)?

Whose example of headship is a husband to follow (v 23)?

What does this mean a husband will do for his wife (v 25)?

Why will it be a positive thing for a wife to submit to this kind of husband, do you think?

⊌ **investigate**

8. What does Paul tell us about men and women, particularly husbands and wives, in 1 Corinthians 11 v 11-12?

⊡ **getting personal**

Husbands, how have you led your wife this week? How have you loved her and cared for her?

Wives, how have you helped your husband this week? How have you loved him and encouraged him to lead?

If you aren't married, how might you use church meetings either to show how great you are, or how attractive you are? Would someone who listened to you or saw you be encouraged to think about how wonderful Christ is, or would you be provoking them to focus on how wonderful you are?

⊡ **apply**

Paul is teaching this church that men and women are equally valuable, and different in the roles they have. There is hierarchy in marriage, just as in the relationship between God the Father and God the Son (v 3, 8-9). There is inter-reliance in marriage, just as in the relationship between God the Father and God the Son (v 11-12).

Cultures swing back and forth in their emphases, over-stressing either hierarchy or inter-reliance—pushing *either* exploitation of women, who are viewed as less valuable, *or* egalitarianism, claiming there is no difference at all between men and women.

9. If you followed your culture's values and beliefs, what would that mean for your:
   • church?

   • marriages?

10. If the Bible's teaching shaped everything, how would that change your:
   • church?

   • marriages?

11. Why is it easier for us to follow the culture of our day than the Bible?

- Why is it easier to follow the culture of a previous generation than the Bible?

12. Read **1 Corinthians 1 v 1**. Why is it better for us to hold to the teachings Paul has "passed ... on to" the church (11 v 2)?

↥ **pray**

Thank God...

for who He is: Father, Son and Spirit. Praise Him for His loving relational nature: for the loving authority of the Father, the loving submission of the Son, and the loving humility of the Spirit.

for what His church is. Praise Him that His church is a place where pride and selfishness have no place. Thank Him that the truths His church are based on are unchanging.

Ask God...

to help you with any parts of this passage you have found difficult to understand, accept or apply.

to show you where you might be using your church as a way to gain prestige, or to gain admirers.

4

1 Corinthians 11 v 17-34
THOUGHTFUL UNITY

The story so far

Paul encouraged the Corinthians to keep running the Christian life by obeying God, and not become complacent about their sin and so risk facing His anger.

Paul warned the church not to use their freedom to love idols, and not to make rules to avoid idols, but simply to love others as Christ loved them.

Despite what culture says, God has designed us to live under and with authority, both in marriages and in the church.

⊕ talkabout

1. What is the point of the Lord's Supper, or Communion? How might we get the way we celebrate it wrong?

⊙ investigate

In Paul's day the Roman world ran on a ten-day calendar, while the Jews (and therefore the Christians) ran on a seven-day calendar. The Christians were committed to meeting together each Sunday, to correspond to the resurrection day of Christ. If they could not meet early in the morning, they would meet at night.

So the wealthy, who did not work, could come early—others, who had least control over their schedules, would not arrive until later.

> **Read 1 Corinthians 11 v 17-22**

> **DICTIONARY**
>
> **Directives (v 17):** commands.

2. Imagine Paul was writing to your church about your Sunday meetings. How would you feel about his words in v 17 and v 20?

3. What is happening in this church? Whose interests come first?

• **Read 1 Corinthians 10 v 17.** How were the Corinthians undermining the purpose of the Lord's Supper?

4. Imagine that the Corinthian church, particularly the wealthier members, had been acting in exactly the opposite way from what they were. What would *that* church meeting have been like?

⮊ **apply**

The Corinthians' partisan spirit and lack of compassion clearly contradicted what they were supposed to be celebrating.

5. What contradictions between what we say we believe and how we actually live can go unchallenged today?

6. How might your church membership thoughtlessly cause divisions between richer and poorer Christians:
• as a whole church body?

• as individuals?

⊡ getting personal

Everything we do as church members needs to help other Christians, and avoid harming them. I find it helpful to remember to have an attitude of JOY: Jesus, Others, Yourself.

How are you putting others' needs before your own within your church fellowship?

Do you need to make an effort to build relationships with others in your congregation who *aren't* just like you? How will you do this?

⊕ investigate

▶ **Read verses 23-34**

7. When we share the Lord's Supper, what do we:
• remember?

DICTIONARY

Covenant (v 25): binding agreement (like a contract).

• underline as the message of Christianity?

• look forward to?

8. How will sharing this meal and thinking of these things enable a church to stay united—rich and poor, old and young, mature and new believer?

optional

⊡ **explore more**

> ❯ **Read Psalm 75 v 8 and Isaiah 51 v 17**

What "cup" is to be drunk, and by whom?

After the supper at which He gave His followers a cup of "the new covenant in my blood" (1 Corinthians 11 v 25), the Lord Jesus went to the Garden of Gethsemane to pray.

> ❯ **Read Matthew 26 v 39-42**

What cup did Jesus drink, so that we might not have to?

Why does Christ need to drink that bitter cup in order to offer us the cup of new and eternal relationship, or "covenant", with God?

Why is it right that the Lord's Supper is kept central in every church?

9. If we contribute to thoughtless division in the church, what does that bring (1 Corinthians 11 v 28-29, 31)?

- How does verse 29 help us to understand what Paul means by "an unworthy manner" (v 27)?

10. How should Christians prepare for sharing the Lord's Supper (v 28)?

11. Why is it good that God disciplines His people when they sin thoughtlessly (v 32)?

⊖ apply

12. In what ways could churches today undermine the importance and the message of the Lord's Supper, without meaning to do so?

13. What should we think about during a Lord's Supper meeting? How might we feel?

⊡ pray

Thank God...

that He does not care more for the rich, or the clever, or the confident.

that at the Lord's Supper we are all equally undeserving, and equally forgiven, and equally blessed.

Ask God...

to help you make real changes if you have realized you are not thoughtfully loving other church members.

to shape your thoughts and emotions next time you come to the Lord's Supper.

5
1 Corinthians 12 v 1-31a
YOUR GIFTS, THEIR GOOD

The story so far

Paul warned the Corinthian church not to use their freedom to love idols, and not to make rules to avoid idols, but simply to love others as Christ loved them.

Despite what culture says, God has designed us to live under and with authority, both in marriages and in the church.

Loving our church means being thoughtful in the way we treat members who are different to us, so we can enjoy the unity that the Lord's Supper displays.

⊕ talkabout

1. Why do people go to church?

⊥ investigate

❯ Read 1 Corinthians 12 v 1-11

It seems that the Corinthians had written to Paul and asked him about "spiritual gifts" (v 1)—*charismata*, gifts God has given to His people through His Spirit.

2. How is it that anyone can stop worshipping "mute idols" (v 2) and accept Jesus as Lord (v 3)?

DICTIONARY

Pagans (v 2): people who don't know the true God.
Manifestation (v 7): sign, outworking.
Interpretation (v 10): translating.
Determines (v 11): decides.

3. What else does the Spirit do for believers (v 4, 7, 11)?

• Why had these "manifestations" been given to the Corinthians (v 7b)?

4. What kinds of gifts does the Spirit give to God's people (v 7-10)?

⊡ apply

5. How is the Bible's view of our gifts different from what the world says about our abilities:
• in where they come from?

• in their purpose?

6. How will remembering the truths of these verses prevent us from using our gifts divisively or selfishly?

"Blood is thicker than water." But the Spirit is thicker than blood!

Do you recognize and enjoy the fellowship of people who are, like you, Spirit-filled Christians? How could you work at living out the closeness and unity God has given you with your Christian brothers and sisters? How will you treat them as family?

⊡ **investigate**

▶ **Read verses 12-31a**

DICTIONARY

Indispensable (v 22): something you can't manage without.

7. What image does Paul use here for the church (v 12-13, 27)?

8. How would verses 14-20 stop some church members from feeling useless?

• How would this stop them from envying the gifts of others in the church?

9. How would verses 21-26 stop some Corinthian Christians from feeling proud of their role and gifts within the church?

In verses 28-30, Paul talks about some of the gifts God has given the church through the ages.

10. It seems the Corinthian church had decided that speaking in ecstatic, non-earthly languages—"tongues"—was a special gift, given to special Christians. What does the order of the gifts he mentions suggest that Paul thought of that view?

• What is the real sign of being a Spirit-filled church (v 26)?

⊡ **explore more**

▶ **Read Ephesians 4 v 7-16**

optional

What are the similar themes in both 1 Corinthians 12 and Ephesians 4?

What happens as God's people use their Jesus-given gifts to do "works of service" (Ephesians 4 v 12-16)?

*All this will take place if "**each** part does its work" (v 16). How is this both exciting and challenging for every individual Christian?*

⊟ **apply**

11. What has this part of 1 Corinthians taught us about why we should go to church?

12. How would you use this passage to respond to the following ideas:
  • "I love playing the piano in my jazz band, but I don't have time to play it in church as well. And anyway, I don't like playing the type of songs my pastor chooses!"

  • "I don't do much at church. There's nothing for me to do, really."

  • "I do a lot for my church. And to be honest, I wish everyone else was a bit more like me. Then we'd really get somewhere!"

  • "Real Christians speak in tongues."

⊡ **getting personal**

> Are you more prone to: envying others' gifts, instead of focusing on using your own, or being proud of your gifts and looking down on others, instead of focusing on serving them?
>
> Are there gifts you're not bothering to use for your church?
>
> Why do *you* go to church?

⬆ pray

Thank God...

for the gifts He has given you; and for the gifts He has chosen not to give you, but to give to others.

Ask God...

to enable you to have the right attitude toward your gifts, and toward the gifts of others.

to see how you can most use your gifts for the good of your church.

6
1 Corinthians 12 v 31b –14 v 40
THE MOST EXCELLENT WAY

The story so far

Despite what culture says, God has designed us to live under and with authority, both in marriages and in the church.

Loving our church means being thoughtful in the way we treat members who are different from us, so we can enjoy the unity that the Lord's Supper displays.

Our gifts and abilities are given by the Holy Spirit, to be used to build up Christ's body, the church.

⊕ talkabout

1. What makes a really good church member?

⊔ investigate

❯ Read 1 Corinthians 12 v 31b – 13 v 13

In v 4-7, Paul describes love, positively and negatively.

2. Pick out a couple of descriptions of love that strike you. What would these look like in everyday life?

> **DICTIONARY**
>
> **Fathom (v 2):** understand.
> **The flames (v 3):** being burned to death for being a Christian.
> **Perseveres (v 7):** keeps going, continues.

3. How impressive-looking is the Christian Paul is describing in verses 1-3?

- This is the kind of believer the Corinthians wanted to be, or saw themselves as. How would these verses shock them?

In verses 8-11, Paul looks forward to when believers die and enter God's presence, or when Christ returns.

4. What contrasts does he draw between our experience as God's people now, and our experience as God's people then?

- How is this exciting? How is it humbling?

⊡ apply

5. How is 1 Corinthians 13 a wonderful passage to use for:
• confession?

• thanksgiving?

• prayer?

• reconciliation?

6. **Read John 13 v 34-35.** What does a loving church do?

• Do people see something different in your church because of your love for each other? How? How not?

⊡ getting personal

Do these characteristics of love describe you? Could you replace the word "love" in verses 4-7 with your own name?

Without this love we are "nothing". Which love-inspired quality do you need to ask the Spirit to grow in you? What words or actions of Jesus will you look at to inspire you? How will you change?

⊕ investigate

❱ Read 1 Corinthians 14 v 1-25

7. Paul talks about "prophecy"—that is, Spirit-led utterances of biblical truth. Why is prophecy better than speaking in tongues in church?
    • v 2-11:

> **DICTIONARY**
>
> **Edifies/edified (v 4, 5, 17):** builds up.
> **Revelation (v 6):** message from God.
> **Intelligible (v 9):** understandable.
> **Unfruitful (v 14):** not doing very much.

    • v 13-17:

    • v 23-25:

⊡ explore more

❱ Re-read verses 20-22

In v 21, Paul quotes from the prophet Isaiah, who was pointing people to a time when God would bring judgment to rebellious people.

What would be the sign that judgment had come (v 21)?

So, when a non-Christian visits a church, what does the "sign" of speaking in unintelligible tongues point to?

But what kind of people does prophecy produce?

▶ Read verses 26-40

8. How should the character of God (v 33) be seen in His people's gatherings:

• v 26?

• v 27-28?

• v 29-33?

• v 34-35? (Note: 11 v 5 indicates that this "silence" is not absolute. It probably relates to shouting out during services to ask questions.)

The Corinthians thought they were "spiritually gifted", mature, Christians.

9. What does Paul say a *truly* mature Christian will do (v 36-40)?

➡ apply

10. How do these chapters help us:
   • not make too *much* of speaking in tongues (or any other particular gift)?

   • not make too *little* of speaking in tongues?

11. What is the most excellent way to be a good church member?

☺ getting personal

How are you going to be a more effective church member:
• in your attitude to meeting together?
• in your actions at the meetings?

↑ pray

Thank God for...

Ask God to...

7 1 Corinthians 15
RESURRECTION: HOLD ON

The story so far

Loving our church means being thoughtful in the way we treat members who are different from us, so we can enjoy the unity that the Lord's Supper displays.

Our gifts and abilities are given by the Holy Spirit, to be used to build up Christ's body, the church.

What matters most is love. Love must guide the way we view our church, and how we use our gifts for our church. Without love, we're nothing.

⊕ talkabout

1. What will life after death be like?

⊕ investigate

> **Read 1 Corinthians 15 v 1-11**

2. What are the essential parts of the gospel message?

DICTIONARY

In vain (v 2): pointlessly.
Scriptures (v 3-4): Paul means what we call the Old Testament.
Fallen asleep (v 6): died.
Abnormally born (v 8): the other apostles knew Jesus before His death, and saw the risen Jesus before He ascended to heaven. Paul met the risen Jesus after His ascension (see Acts 9 v 1-19).

• Why can we be confident that Christ "was raised"?

3. How do the Corinthians need to relate to this gospel message, and why (v 2)?

☐ apply

4. Today, how do people and even churches alter the various parts of the true, apostolic gospel message?

• Why do even small changes to the gospel matter? How should we respond?

☐ investigate

Some of the Corinthians were altering the gospel message by saying there was no resurrection from the dead (v 12).

> Read verses 12-34

5. Why does this matter (v 13-18, 29-32)?

• If there is no resurrection, what are Christians (v 19)?

• If there is no resurrection, why is the saying Paul quotes at the end of verse 32 the sensible way to live?

"But Christ has indeed been raised" (v 20)—which means the opposite of verses 13-18 and 29-32 is actually true!

6. Work back through those verses and pick out why the fact of Jesus' resurrection is such good news.

7. What does the resurrection guarantee about the future:
   • for Christians (v 23)?

   • for everything (v 24-28)?

➔ apply

8. How should the reality of the resurrection change our lives?

   • Why is it tempting to live as though the end of verse 32 were ultimate reality?

😀 getting personal

Paul warns us that bad company corrupts and misleads us (v 33). Do you make sure you have friends who will remind you of the reality of the resurrection, and encourage you by pointing you to your future? How could you start doing this, or do this more, for your Christian friends?

⊕ investigate

Even for those first-century people who believed in immortality, the idea of bodily resurrection was unattractive, unthinkable, and just plain weird. So, they asked: "How are the dead raised? With what kind of body will they come?" (v 35).

❯ Read verses 35-58

9. How will our resurrection "spiritual" bodies be different from our "natural" bodies now?
   • v 42-44:

DICTIONARY

Sow (v 36) / sown (v 42-44): plant a seed.
Perishable / imperishable (v 42, 50, 52-54): facing death / everlasting.
Natural (v 44, 46): here, it means earthly and sinful, and dying.
Spiritual (v 44, 46): heavenly and eternal (it doesn't mean "not physical").

   • v 50-54:

10. How does our sin make death painful—something that "stings" (v 56)?

   • How does the gospel message (v 3-8) show us that death now has no sting for Christians?

⊡ explore more

▶ Read Genesis 2 v 7 and Daniel 7 v 13

Where does the first man, Adam, come from?

How about the "son of man" in Daniel's God-given vision?

This is the point Paul is making in 1 Corinthians 15 v 47.

What does being "in Adam", or like Adam, mean for us (1 Corinthians 15 v 21-22, 48-49)?

Why is it wonderful to be "in Christ", made like Him through faith in Him (v 21-22, 48-49)?

⊟ apply

11. As Christians, how should we view death?

12. What does Paul want us to do between now and our deaths (v 58)?

13. Why is the resurrection important?

⊡ **getting personal**

"Jesus … for the joy set before him endured the cross, scorning its shame, and sat down at the right hand of the throne of God" (Hebrews 12 v 2).

Do you keep the joy of your resurrected life before your eyes each day? How could you remind yourself of it at home, at work, when you wake up and when you go to bed?

How will your guaranteed future cause you to live like Christ now, sacrificing your interests and enduring suffering to love others?

⊞ **pray**

Spend some time **thanking God** for raising the Lord Jesus from the dead. Use the passage to thank God for what the resurrection means for you as Christians.

Speak to God about the ways He has given you to labor for Him. **Ask Him** to help you work joyfully in His service. Tell Him when you find this hard!

8 1 Corinthians 16
GOOD EXAMPLES

The story so far

Our gifts and abilities are given by the Holy Spirit, to be used to build up Christ's body, the church.

What matters most is love. Love must guide the way we view our church, and how we use our gifts for our church. Without love, we're nothing.

The resurrection is part of the gospel, and the basis for our future hope and our present hard work. We must hold firmly to its truth!

⊕ talkabout

1. How do people suggest struggling churches can be turned around?

⊕ investigate

2. What have been the main points of Paul's teaching in this letter to a struggling church?

▶ Read 1 Corinthians 16 v 1-20

3. What does Paul say about how this local church should relate to churches elsewhere?

⊡ explore more

optional

Paul wants them to "set aside a sum of money in keeping with his income" to give to other, less wealthy, Christians (v 1-2).

▶ Read 2 Corinthians 8 v 7-15 and 9 v 7-11

What further guidelines about Christian financial giving are given here?

Why do we give up our comfort to give money to others (8 v 9; 9 v 8)?

Why do many Christians find it hard to see their finances as Paul does, do you think?

4. What do we see in 1 Corinthians 16 about Paul's own priorities?

5. Who does Paul mention as examples of Christ-like living? What do you think he wants the Corinthian Christians to learn from each of them?

➔ apply

6. If the people mentioned in this passage were members of your church today, what would they be doing and saying?

• How would they be challenging you?

⊕ investigate

❯ Read verses 13-14 and 21-24

7. How does verse 13 help us understand what it looks like to obey Paul's command in verse 14?

• Think of the problems this church was struggling with. How would obeying Paul's words here turn the church around?

8. How does verse 22 help us understand what it looks like to obey v 14?

⊡ **getting personal**

Christian love is no mere abstract theory; it is not a disembodied, unengaged cheerfulness, like some drug-induced state. Christian love calls us not to desert but to stand guard, not to give up but to stand firm, not to avoid conflict in cowardice but to defend truth in courage. Christian love is not about a yielding weakness but a persevering strength. Most of all, it is about loving the Christ who has loved us perfectly in this way.

In which parts of your life can you be encouraged by your strong love?

Where do you need to start loving others in a Christian way? How will you start doing this?

9. Verse 22 is a warning. Why is verse 23 such good news for flawed churches and flawed Christians (that is, you and me)?

Think again about how these Christians were treating others within their church, treating Paul, and treating the gospel of Christ.

10. Why is verse 24 an astonishing way for Paul to finish his letter? What does it tell us about Paul?

→ **apply**

11. What are the areas covered in 1 Corinthians which your church most needs to hear?

• How could you help your church to become more like Paul's goal for the Corinthian church?

↑ **pray**

Thank God...

for His grace.

for the ways in which His Spirit has encouraged you from His word in 1 Corinthians (be specific).

Ask God to...

help you change to be more loving members of your church (again, be specific about things you need to start doing, or do more or less of).

Leader's Guide: 1 Corinthians 10 – 16

INTRODUCTION

Leading a Bible study can be a bit like herding cats—everyone has a different idea of what the passage could be about, and a different line of enquiry that they want to pursue. But a good group leader is more than someone who just referees this kind of discussion. You will want to:

• correctly understand and handle the Bible passage. But also…

• encourage and train the people in your group to do this for themselves. Don't fall into the trap of spoon-feeding people by simply passing on the information in the Leader's Guide. Then…

• make sure that no Bible study is finished without everyone knowing how the passage is relevant for them. What changes do you all need to make in light of the things you have been learning? And finally…

• encourage the group to turn all that has been learned and discussed into prayer.

Your Bible-study group is unique, and you are likely to know better than anyone the capabilities, backgrounds and circumstances of the people you are leading. That's why we've designed these guides with a number of optional features. If they're a quiet bunch, you might want to spend longer on talkabout. If your time is limited, you can choose to skip explore more, or get people to look at these questions at home. Can't get enough of Bible study? Well, some studies have optional extra homework projects. As leader, you can adapt and select the material to the needs of your particular group.

So what's in the Leader's Guide?
The main thing that this Leader's Guide will help you to do is to understand the major teaching points in the passage you are studying, and how to apply them. As well as guidance on the questions, the Leader's Guide for each session contains the following important sections:

THE BIG IDEA

One key sentence will give you the main point of the session. This is what you should be aiming to have fixed in people's minds as they leave the Bible study. And it's the point you need to head back toward when the discussion goes off on a tangent.

SUMMARY

An overview of the passage, including plenty of useful historical background information.

OPTIONAL EXTRA

Usually this is an introductory activity that ties in with the main theme of the Bible study, and is designed to "break the ice" at the beginning of a session. Or it may be a "homework project" that people can tackle during the week.

So let's take a look at the various different features of a Good Book Guide:

⊕ talkabout

Each session kicks off with a discussion question, based on the group's opinions or experiences. It's designed to get people talking and thinking in a general way about the main subject of the Bible study.

⬇ investigate

The first thing you and your group need to know is what the Bible passage is about, which is the purpose of these questions. But watch out—people may come up with answers based on their experiences or teaching they have heard in the past, without referring to the passage at all. It's amazing how often we can get through a Bible study without actually looking at the Bible! If you're stuck for an answer, the Leader's Guide contains guidance on questions. These are the answers to direct your group to. This information isn't meant to be read out to people—ideally, you want them to discover these answers from the Bible for themselves. Sometimes there are optional follow-up questions (see ⊗ in guidance on questions) to help you help your group get to the answer.

⊡ explore more

These questions generally point people to other relevant parts of the Bible. They are useful for helping your group to see how the passage fits into the "big picture" of the whole Bible. These sections are OPTIONAL—only use them if you have time. Remember that it's better to finish in good time having really grasped one big thing from the passage, than to try and cram everything in.

➔ apply

We want to encourage you to spend more time working at application—too often, it is simply tacked on at the end. In the Good Book Guides, apply sections are mixed in with the investigate sections of the study. We hope that people will realize that application is not just an optional extra, but rather, the whole purpose of studying the

Bible. We do Bible study so that our lives can be changed by what we hear from God's word. If you skip the application, the Bible study hasn't achieved its purpose.

These questions draw out practical lessons that we can all learn from the Bible passage. You can review what has been learned so far, and think about practical differences that this should make in our churches and our lives. The group gets the opportunity to talk about what they personally have learned.

⬇ getting personal

These can be done at home, but it is well worth allowing a few moments of quiet reflection during the study for each person to think and pray about specific changes they need to make in their own lives. Why not have a time for reporting back at the beginning of the following session, so that everyone can be encouraged and challenged by one another to make application a priority?

⬆ pray

In Acts 4 v 25-30 the first Christians quoted Psalm 2 as they prayed in response to the persecution of the apostles by the Jewish religious leaders. Today however, it's not as common for Christians to base prayers on the truths of God's word as it once was. As a result, our prayers tend to be weak, superficial and self-centered rather than bold, visionary and God-centered.

The prayer section is based on what has been learned from the Bible passage. How different our prayer times would be if we were genuinely responding to what God has said to us through His word.

1

1 Corinthians 9 v 24 – 10 v 14
KEEP ON RUNNING

THE BIG IDEA
God warns us that we need to keep going as His people by avoiding complacency about our sin.

SUMMARY
The church Paul had established in Corinth was young, full of life, and just as full of problems. At the time of Paul's letter, it was threatened with self-destruction. But its members did not realize this. Overconfidence in themselves and complacency about their relationship with God meant they needed to be warned about the reality of God's judgment of sin—judgment on those who call themselves His people as well as those who know they are not.

So, having encouraged the Corinthian Christians to keep running to get the prize of eternal life with God (9 v 24-25), Paul points them to an example to avoid: the Israelites in the time of the exodus and journey to the promised land (10 v 1-10). They had known great blessings from God and were well acquainted with His power. But even so they disobeyed God, and did not turn back to Him. And so they came under God's judgment—they died in the desert (v 5). They had crossed the starting line, but did not reach the finish line.

They are an example to the Corinthians (v 6, 11)—a warning of God's judgment on sin. Complacency—assuming we're standing firm—can easily lead to us falling (v 12). God will enable us to resist any temptation—no temptation is unendurable (v 13). So therefore, no giving in to temptation is excusable. We can, and must, obey God.

Since this is the first study in this Good Book Guide focusing on the second half of the letter, Q7 takes your group to a few verses outlining how the Corinthian church had fallen into a pattern of disobedience to how God wanted them to live. We need to take note of the examples both of Israel and of the Corinthian church, and learn not to make the same mistakes. Our churches cannot coast along in spiritual things. And, individually, whether or not we have been baptized, take communion, or see God's blessing in our lives, we need to continue humbly to obey God, and ensure we don't become complacent and slip into unnoticed, unrepentant sin. We have crossed the starting line—we need to keep running in order to reach the finish line and receive the "crown that will last forever" (9 v 25).

OPTIONAL EXTRA
Before the study, get your group to read 1 Corinthians 1 v 1 – 9 v 23. Ask them to pick out truths about God the Father and God the Son, and to come up with a one-sentence description of the church in Corinth that Paul was writing to.

GUIDANCE TO QUESTIONS
1. Imagine the starting line of a popular marathon. The starter's pistol goes, and the runners set off. Which of them are really marathon runners? In one sense, all of them. In another, possibly none of them—or at least, we can't know! All runners in a marathon are marathon runners—unless they don't finish. Then, they were in fact never marathon runners, because they didn't run a marathon. It's only

once someone finishes a marathon that we know they were marathon runners all along. The starting line and the finish line are not the same thing! Allow your group to discuss and disagree with one another! You could refer back to this question after Q7 and ask: What things threaten the Corinthian Christians so that they no longer keep running the Christian race?

2. What period is [Paul] focusing on (10 v 1-4)? The time when the Israelites were rescued from Egypt by God, who then parted the Red Sea for them to escape through (Exodus 13 v 17 – 14 v 31) and led them through the desert toward the promised land.

- **What advantages did these people have (v 1-4)? Note:** If your group is unfamiliar with the events of the exodus, use the Explore More section below before answering this question.
  - "Under the cloud and passed through the sea"—they were led by God through the Red Sea.
  - "Baptized into Moses" (v 2)—they were members of the people who were under the leadership of Moses, God's chosen leader. His deliverance was their deliverance—what he achieved, they achieved.
  - They ate "spiritual food" and "drank spiritual drink"—God gave them miraculous food and water.
  - The rock they drank from "was Christ" (v 4)—the rock from which the Israelites drank physical water symbolized Christ. Paul seems to mean that the Son of God was spiritually sustaining them.

- **Read Exodus 17 v 5-6. What does Paul say was happening spiritually as they were given physical food and drink by God?** They were feeding on Christ. As people who trusted in God's promises, they were sustained spiritually by their dependance on the Christ who God had promised would come.

EXPLORE MORE
Read Exodus 14 v 21-31; 16 v 4-5, 13-18; 17 v 5-6. How do these passages help us appreciate how blessed these people were? God was working powerfully and miraculously on their behalf, day by day. They had received so much from God—rescue, food, water—without which they would have died, and which they had no hope of providing for themselves.

3. What is the shock in [1 Cor 10] verse 5? "Their bodies were scattered all over the desert". Numbers 13 – 14 give the background to this statement—it is worth reading beforehand and summarizing to your group. Even after all that blessing, God killed some of them. Despite an amazing start to their life as God's people, many of them did not continue as God's people.

- **Why did this happen (v 6-10)?**
  - v 6: they set their hearts on evil.
  - v 7: they were "idolators", copying the religious practices of "pagan" (ie: non-God-knowing) nations around them.
  - v 8: they committed sexual immorality
  - v 9: they tested the Lord, to see if He really cared.
  - v 10: they grumbled against God, suggesting He didn't know what He was doing, or would not get them to the land He'd promised them.

EXPLORE MORE
Read Exodus 31 v 18 – 32 v 6; Numbers 25 v 1-2; 17 v 1-3. How do

these passages help us appreciate the seriousness of the people's disobedience? In Exodus 32, Israel is at the foot of Mount Sinai, as Moses is given the law by God, which will teach them how to live in the land He's bringing them to. And they spend their time making a god who they then pretend rescued them from Egypt! In Numbers 25, the men leave their wives to commit sexual immorality with women from a different nation, and end up worshipping their gods—all in direct disobedience to God (see Exodus 34 v 15-16). And in Exodus 17, we see them, having just been rescued from slavery, passed through the Red Sea, and eaten food given miraculously, suggesting that God isn't looking after them, and slavery and genocide in Egypt would have been a better option than being part of God's people.

What would these sins look like if they happened in your church fellowship?

4. What does 1 Corinthians 10 v 1-10 tell us about God?

- He is a God of mighty acts, and He uses His might to rescue people.
- He sustains His people, physically and spiritually.
- He works through His chosen leader to deliver His people.
- He is not pleased with people who are disobedient, untrusting, or selfish ie: sinful.
- He punishes people for unrepentant sin—even if they have called themselves His own people.
- He considers idolatry, sexual immorality, untrusting "testing", and grumbling to be sinful.

- **And about following Him?** We need to trust God, keep trusting God, and obey and be guided by Him. We must not think that, because we have been

baptized, or once professed faith, or receive Communion, or have known great blessing from God, that we can persist in disobedient sin.

5. APPLY: Why did Paul include these verses in his letter (v 6, 11)? As examples to teach us not to set our "hearts on evil things" (v 6). The Old Testament was pointing forwards to Christ, who is its fulfillment (v 11)—but God deals with His people in the same way today as He did then. We should learn from the sad example of these people, who fell from the faith. We should avoid their fate by avoiding their sins, or by turning back to God as our ruler and forgiver if ever we commit them.

6. APPLY: In what ways do we excuse giving into temptation? Our excuses vary depending on the temptation and our characters—allow your group to discuss this question. Some possibilities:

- It's not really a sin, so it doesn't matter.
- It is a sin, but only a small one—not a big one like murder or adultery.
- I just couldn't resist.
- There was no way out. I had no choice.
- You don't know what I face. Anyone in my position would give in.

How does verse 13 encourage and challenge us? The *encouragement* is that God will enable us to resist any temptation. We only face things that tempt other people too—and though we will not be able to avoid temptation, by God's grace we will never face a temptation that is unendurable. He will always make us able to obey Him. In thinking about the *challenge*, you could take each excuse your group has come up with, and find the answer to that excuse in these verses. For those above:

- God defines what sin is. We're not at liberty to redefine it (v 6-10).

- There is no small sin. God punishes it (v 5).
- We can always resist—God never allows us to be tempted unendurably (v 13).
- God always provides a way out. There is always an option which does not involve sinning (v 13).
- We don't face a temptation that no one else has faced (v 13).

7. In pairs or on your own, pick out the areas in which this church was facing, or giving into, temptation.
- 1 v 11-12: Being divisive and argumentative; following and being loyal to a minister, rather than to Christ.
- 3 v 3: Being envious of other Christians.
- 4 v 18: Being arrogant, assuming they knew better than an apostle such as Paul.
- 5 v 1-2: Sexual immorality (eg: sleeping with close relations)—and pride about tolerating and accepting this behavior.
- 6 v 6-7: Suing one another in court.
- 8 v 8-13: (This one is tricky!) Doing things that Christians are free to do without thinking about the impact this has on the faith of other Christians who may think it's wrong, and so be encouraged to do something they believe to be sinful.

8. Read 4 v 10. How does Paul describe this church's view of him, and of themselves? The Corinthian church saw Paul as a fool, weak, and dishonored. They, on the other hand, were (they thought) wise, strong and honored.

- **How does this match what you saw in Q7?** The Corinthian church was certainly not wise or strong, and deserved no honor! They were backbiting and selfish, proud and complacent, and praising of sinful behavior. The reality God saw in this church was very different from how they liked to see themselves.

9. Why did this church need to hear verse 12? Because they were overconfident. They thought they were standing firm, and so were not noticing or dealing with the disobedience that had spread through so many areas of their church's life. And so they were in danger of "falling"—of coming under God's judgment instead of enjoying His blessing and salvation.

- **Why did they need to hear the warning of what happened to the Israelites in Moses' day?** Because being church members, calling themselves Christians, receiving baptism and taking communion provide no final security against God's judgment for a life lived in unrepentant licentiousness. The Israelites had considered themselves God's people, but had fallen under punishment for their sin—this church needed to take care they did not face the same end.

10. APPLY: Why is complacency— thinking "you are standing firm"—such a danger to a church? Complacency can very easily lead (as it had in Corinth) to sinful behaviour, and therefore to a "fall"—to not finishing the Christian race, and missing out on the crown that will last eternally (9 v 25). And if a church is complacent, it won't notice a slow, steady decline into disobedience, until it is too late. The time we are most likely to "fall" is when we assume we are "standing firm".

11. APPLY: What are the greatest challenges your church faces when it comes to obeying God? Encourage your group to include themselves in this discussion (we often find it easier to notice how others are not obeying God). You might like to use the answers to Q3 and Q7 as a basis for your discussion.

2 1 Corinthians 10 v 14 – 11 v 1
LOVE, LIBERTY AND LEGALISM

THE BIG IDEA
The Christian life is about loving as Christ loves: not about using our freedom to love idols, nor making rules to avoid idols.

SUMMARY
The idea of laying aside our rights in order to serve and help others has been underlying Paul's words since 8 v 1. Paul brings this point to a conclusion in this section.

Here we find that the Christian life is not a life of legalism. Neither is it a life of self-indulgence. It is a Christ-like life, marked supremely by self-sacrificial love, and lived out for the good of others. We are to live for the glory (or we might say the good) of God (10 v 31). And we do this by broadcasting His love in Christ—which is also for the good of others (v 33). We're to act in a way which avoids causing others to misunderstand the gospel (v 32). This is how Paul lived (11 v 1), because that's how Christ lived—and how the Corinthian Christians, and God's people today, are to live too!

Living this life requires us to avoid two errors. One is to flee false gods (10 v 14). Christian freedom does not mean we are free to do as we choose, or to follow what the world around us does. Paul argues that worshipping an idol is actually worshipping a demon (10 v 20). These Christians could not participate both in the worship of the Lord and of demons.

Second is to avoid legalism. There are times when Christians shouldn't do things they are free to (as Paul has already said in 8 v 9-13, and does again here in 10 v 23-28). But the correct response to a situation where Christians should curtail their freedom to

make the gospel message clear is not the establishing of a law, a rule which Christians "must" follow. Paul doesn't want our actions to spring from following some extra-biblical rule. But he does want our actions to be directed by love, so that the way we use, or don't use, our Christian freedoms is dictated by what brings glory to God and is for the good of others.

This session is in two broad sections. The first focuses more on worshipping the true God and avoiding idolatry; the second, on living for the glory of the true God and avoiding legalism. And we need to listen to Paul and apply his words no less today than in first-century Corinth. Idol-feasts and eating meat sacrificed to idols may not be issues we face, or ways in which we could tip into idolatry or legalism. But compromising our faith to worship other things, and making extra rules which we then insist Christians keep, are no less dangers for us than they were for the Corinthians!

GUIDANCE TO QUESTIONS
1. What expectations can Christians lay on each other which are not found in the Bible? Why do you think Christians do this? This is a hard question, and answers will vary depending on your church and your society. Some possibilities are:
- Not drinking alcohol.
- Going to church a specified number of times on a Sunday.
- Not wearing particular items of clothing
- Listening to, or not listening to, particular types of music.
- a daily "quiet time" with a particular structure.

• **What issues that the Bible is clear on can Christians often ignore? Why do you think Christians do this?** Again, this will vary depending on where your church is. Encourage your group to think of things they often want to ignore, rather than only things they've noticed other church members tending to ignore!

Note: It might be that you come up with answers here that the Bible actually doesn't give a rule about. In which case, this is, ironically, an answer to the first part of this question. Avoid spending a long time on issues upon which biblical Christians respectfully disagree (Sabbath observance, infant baptism, etc).

2. What is Paul's clear command in verse 14? Flee the false gods! He says it urgently, in much the same tone as his earlier exhortation to flee from sexual immorality (6 v 18). Paul was urging the Corinthian Christians not to eat in the pagan temples or at the public feasts.

3. What does he say we are doing when we share the Lord's Supper?
(1) Participating in the body and blood of Christ (v 16). The point here seems to be the effect of sharing the wine and bread. To receive them rightly—that is, with true faith—is to receive Christ, to share in the benefits of His saving work on the cross. Taking Communion doesn't save us. Trusting in Christ and His death proclaimed in the supper does.
(2) Uniting around the cross of Christ (v 17). The Lord's Supper demonstrates that Christ's blood spilled and body broken are the center of our fellowship with each other. Participating in one loaf makes us one people, with one Lord.

• **A lot of Corinthian social and political**

life had to do with great public feasts held at pagan temples, where the food had been offered to false gods. **What does Paul say is really happening at these feasts (v 19-20)?** Though the idols themselves are nothing (v 19, see also 8 v 4), behind the idols stand demons (v 20). Paul is treating idols as the prophets of the Old Testament did (see Explore More below on Deuteronomy 32 v 10-22, and also Psalm 106 v 37).

4. What choice do Christians have to make (v 21)? Paul reasons that the Corinthians could not participate in the worship of both the Lord (seen most clearly in the Lord's Supper) and of demons (ie: worshipping idols, seen most clearly in the pagan temple feasts). Doing both is an impossibility.
Christians today equally have to keep deciding not to worship idols/demons, but rather to worship our one Lord. Flee idolatry, Paul says.

EXPLORE MORE
Read Deut 32 v 10-22. What had God done for "him" ie: Israel (v 10-14)? The image is from the animal kingdom, of an eagle looking after a young one. God had found Israel, shielded and cared for "him", led him, and given him a place to live of safety and plenty.
What did Jeshurun (a term for Israel) do in response (v 15-18)? They took everything God had given them (v 15), and then rejected Him (v 15), worshipping other "gods" (v 16). They forgot all about the God who had given them everything (v 18).
How do verses 16-17 link with our 1 Cor passage? Israel worshipped idols (v 16), which in fact was sacrificing to demons (v 17). Paul tells the Corinthian church this is what they're doing if they join in idol feasts.

What was God's response? He was jealous (jealousy is not the same as envy. Envy is wanting something someone else has been given. Jealousy is wanting something that is rightfully yours, but that someone else has taken. If a wife leaves her husband for another man, he has every right to be jealous.) And he was angry (v 16).

How is this a warning both to the Corinthian Christians, and to us, when it comes to idolatry? Idolatry brings God's judgment on us. We need to be careful—we can't survive a confrontation with God when He is against us, and idolatry sets us against Him. We need to admit our sin and ask for forgiveness.

5. APPLY: What are the most-worshiped idols in your culture? Why are they attractive? You might like to use the questions in Getting Personal on page 15 to identify common false gods. The aim here is both to identify the idols that surround you as Christians, and to see why they seem attractive. Encourage your group to dig deeper than the surface. Eg: we may think that our car is our idol—the thing that excites us and we daydream about—when in fact it is status that is our idol, and the car is the means to serving that "god".

6. APPLY: How might a Christian in your church end up trying to worship both God and one of these idols? How does this part of 1 Cor warn them? Use the answers to the first part of Q5 in your discussion here. This passage warns us that there is not room for both God and an idol to be Lord of our hearts. It must be one, or the other. If we do not flee from idols, we are not truly worshipping the one true God.

7. What does Paul say about [eating meat which has been sacrificed to idols], and why (v 25-26, 30)? Christians have the freedom to eat anything. So the Corinthians were free to eat anything sold in the market, even though it had most likely come from sacrifices offered in one of the city temples. That does not matter, though, because, says Paul (citing Psalm 24 v 1); "The earth is the Lord's, and everything in it" (v 26). This was a well-known verse among first-century Jews, and was recited by many before eating. The point is that God alone is the source of all of the meat. When Paul himself eats such meat in a private setting, he is worshipping God by giving thanks to Him for it, not worshipping a demon (v 30)!

8. But it isn't always fine to eat meat that's been sacrificed! When wouldn't it be (v 28-29a)? When eating the meat would appear to be approving of idol-worship, because you're eating it with a non-Christian who has told you that the meat you are about to eat has been sacrificed to an idol.

• **Why not?! If someone who worships idols sees Christians eating meat that's been sacrificed to idols, what might they think about Christianity?** Eating the meat might confuse non-believers about the gospel. They might think that Christianity includes idol worship—that Jesus is just another addition to the pantheon of pagan gods, rather than the Son of God, unique and supreme. Or they may end up thinking that Christian belief makes no difference to how the Christian believer actually lives.

9. So, if it's not following a rule or enjoying freedom, what should direct a Christian's actions (v 31-32)? Living for God's glory in everything we do. We glorify God by acknowledging and displaying His character, His actions, His holiness, His love. We broadcast His love in Christ.

So part of bringing glory to God involves enabling others to see His glory. A Christian's actions are directed by a desire not to act in any way which causes people to misunderstand who God is, and what Christ has done (v 32)—whether Jews, non-Jews, or other Christians. In Corinth, the desire to glorify God by showing and sharing Christ with others should outweigh their desire to enjoy their liberty to eat any meat.

10. Whose good is Paul seeking? What is his primary aim for them (v 33)? Not his own, by simply enjoying his freedom, or liberty—but the good of others, giving up his liberty where necessary out of love for those around him. His aim is that they may be saved. This is what is best for them, and what brings glory to God—which is Paul's highest aim in life (v 31).

Note: Verse 32 doesn't mean we live to please others, either for the sake of our own self-advancement, nor simply to bring them pleasure. "We must obey God rather than men" (Acts 5 v 29). We are always to consider God first (v 31).

• **In 11 v 1, Paul says he's following "the example of Christ". Read Luke 19 v 1-10. What does Paul mean?** Christ said He came to *seek* the lost so that He could *save* them (Luke 19 v 10). These are the two words Paul uses in 1 Corinthians 10 v 32. He *seeks* not his own good but the good of others, so that they might come to Jesus and be *saved*.

Christ is our example; Paul tries to be like Christ. Just as Jesus did, he curtails his own liberty so he can love others and love God. We should follow Paul, and those we know who seek others' good, so that non-Christians might be saved by coming

to faith—because people who do this are following the example of Christ Himself.

11. APPLY: How is acting legalistically different from acting out of love? Making an absolute rule which the Bible does not, and then keeping it, is doing something which allows us to feel we are good, or doing well. The motivation of a legalist, who is concerned with keeping rules (and insisting that others do), is self-centered. We don't act out of thoughtful love for another, or for God—in fact, we act for ourselves, building up our own sense of pride in our performance.

• **Is it possible to end up making an idol out of keeping religious rules? How?** An idol is something we trust and serve as the thing which will give us what we need. So, strange though it sounds, we can make religious rules (even God's perfect law itself!) into an idol if we think that by serving, or keeping, those rules, we will get a good life now, and a good life eternally. We end up not serving God, or loving Him, but rather serving some rules, out of love for ourselves.

12. APPLY: Think of some real-life circumstances where acting out of love for others means giving up your Christian liberty. Of course, your group will come up with their own ideas, but some examples could include:

• not publicly supporting a particular political party if we realize it will lead to others thinking that all of that party's policies are Christian—or that Christianity is that party's platform.

• not drinking alcohol with non-Christians who simply see drinking alcohol as a way to get drunk.

• not spending our money on a brand new

car (which we're free to do as Christians) because we know that our neighbors make idols of having the latest model, and we don't want to suggest that we are driven by the same desires.

Note: This is not being "ascetic"—rejecting the possession and enjoyment of things for its own sake. All things are created by God and are to be enjoyed if we do so in a thankful way (1 Timothy 4 v 4). It is freely choosing to give up what is good and can be enjoyed, because we want to help others understand the gospel.

• **How could we end up being legalistic in those situations?**
  • Saying Christians mustn't enter politics, or be members of political parties; banning politics from church.
  • Making a rule that drinking alcohol is always wrong.
  • Saying that Christians should never buy a new car, period.

3 1 Corinthians 11 v 2-16
LOVING AUTHORITY

THE BIG IDEA:

God has designed us to live under and with authority—we need to welcome this in our churches and marriages, regardless of what our culture says.

SUMMARY

This is a famously difficult passage! The key theme is noticing the relationships that we live in as Christians, and how God has designed this world to have hierarchical structure and interdependence, or mutuality. Western society pushes autonomy—literally, self-law—as the way to live, so that we free ourselves from all idea of living under authority, and give up any idea of being in responsible authority ourselves. Paul wants us to see the inadequacy of autonomy as a way to understand following Christ.

To understand Paul's teaching, we must understand the cultural context of first-century Corinth: how people displayed messages through what they wore. In Corinth, women discarded head coverings to indicate that they wanted there to be no distinction made between them and men (particularly their husbands); and to indicate they were at liberty sexually (to be unfaithful, if they were married). To show their social status, wealthy and respected men would pull over their heads a portion of their best toga when leading prayer in the pagan temples and at the great public feasts.

So Paul says that whenever a woman prays in a public meeting, she should cover her head. Women were not to use church meetings to give the appearance of immorality. And when Paul exhorts the men to pray with their heads uncovered, he is wanting them to communicate humility, rather than arrogance.

Instead, wives are to be under their husband's authority, both in church settings and in their marriages, which is where the second half of this study focuses. God's plan, seen in Genesis 1 – 2 and underlined here, is for men and women to live together in marriage as equal and different partners. The man leads; the woman helps. But (as we see in the Explore More section) a husband's leadership is to be Christ-like ie: loving, other-person-focused, sacrificial. And a woman's submission is also to be Christ-like, because Jesus is a faithful Son who always does the Father's will, without this ever denigrating Him or His dignity.

Verses 8-10 are balanced by verses 11-12. Because men might easily distort the teaching Paul was giving here, he adds that men and women need each other; we are interdependent. This is how God made us, to bear one another's burdens. We find it in friendships when we help each other, sometimes despite—many times because of—our differences, especially in marriage.

All of this is very counter-cultural if you live in the west. Our societies are egalitarian— teaching that men and women, if they are to be equal in value, must be equal in role (conveniently ignoring the biological fact that only women can carry and give birth to a child!). Biblical churches and marriages are complementarian—teaching that men and women are equal in value because the "come from God" (v 12), and different in role. The study finishes with a reminder that Paul, as an appointed apostle chosen by the Creator God, has authority to say how we should live in this world that trumps any human society or culture.

Note: For a good, biblical and more in-depth look at these issues, read *Recovering Biblical Manhood and Womanhood: A Response to Evangelical Feminism*, edited John Piper and Wayne Grudem.

GUIDANCE ON QUESTIONS

1. When is "authority" a good thing? When is it bad? It is hard for us today to hear of authority without immediately thinking of a negative authoritarianism. But we do regularly experience the blessing of being under good authority. Encourage your group to think of examples of loving, caring authority that provides safety and happiness in the workplace, in the family home, and on a national level—and to think of instances where authority in these places can be exploitative and selfish.

- **What gives one person the right to have authority over another?** If we do not answer "Because God has given it", we struggle to find a reason for one person to have authority. As your group discuss this, you may want to challenge them to find reasons that aren't "Because God has given it". Possibilities include the will of the people; being stronger and being able to impose your will; or that no one has the right. For each, tease out the problems: what if the people get it wrong? Does being stronger really infer a right to authority? What would happen if there really were no authority in our country?!

2. What is the relationship between wife and husband (v 3)? The husband is the "head" of a marriage, in his role. The idea of "head" here is about authority— "headship" means "being over".
Which other relationship does this reflect? The relationship that lies at the core of biblical thinking about gender and marriage is the relationship between the Father and the Son. Understanding the relational aspects of the Trinity gives us insight into understanding gender roles. God the Father and Son are equal in personhood and importance—in value (see John 10 v 30; 17 v 21-24). So, too, are men and women, husbands and wives. At the same time, there is a difference in roles between God the Father and God the Son (see 1 Corinthians 3 v 23; 15 v 27-28; John 4 v 34; 5 v 30; 6 v 38). So too between husband and wife.

Note: This is a controversial topic! You may want to look at the Explore More section, which takes us to Ephesians 5 v 22-33, at this stage, instead of after Q7.

3. Why would a man doing this [ie: covering his head with his toga] in church be dishonoring his "head" (v 3-4)? Because instead of his praying or prophesying pointing people to how great Jesus (his "head") is, he is pointing to his own status and greatness. Paul is attacking the practice of a man covering his head not because it is wrong *per se*, but because it represents an autonomous arrogance, rather than displaying humility as one under the authority of Christ.

• **What were men using their roles in the church service to do?** This reinforces the previous part of this question. They were behaving like this to gain glory for themselves, to show how good they were—rather than humbly pointing people to Christ, to glorify Him.

4. How does this [ie: covered hair showing you were married] help us understand why Paul says what he does in verse 5-6? Women discarded their head coverings to indicate that they were not under their husband's authority, not bound by their wedding vows. Today, the cultural equivalent would be to remove your wedding ring in an obvious way. A woman with an uncovered head and loose, flowing hair was saying: *I am sexually available to you, and I would like you to look at me with this in mind.* And so Paul says that whenever a woman prays in a public meeting, she should cover her head.

• **What were women (especially married ones) using their roles in church services to do?** To advertise themselves

as potentially sexually promiscuous women. To encourage men to think about them, their beauty and potential availability, rather than to encourage men (and other women) to think about Christ, under whose authority they are. To flaunt their freedom.

5. APPLY: What would a church where these things were happening today look like? This will depend on your culture. The question is: what is your society's equivalent of a man pulling his toga over his head, or a woman uncovering and loosening her hair? Some ideas:
For men: deliberately wearing expensive clothing when leading in church; mentioning what they do for a living while praying or prophesying; using humor because we want others to see we are funny (as opposed to making the teaching about Christ clearer or more memorable).
For women: wearing clothing or make-up that we hope will make us physically attractive to men, so that they will notice us and think about us in a sexual way. But it's possible to be motivated by the same desire to be attractive and suggestive, while wearing more modest clothing than that.

6. APPLY: What would be the impact of both these attitudes and behaviors be on a church fellowship? *Division and discord.* Christ will not be glorified by men who point to themselves. Christ's authority will be undermined or ignored. And outsiders will not be attracted to Christ. If we are honest, we must admit that today many people do not think of Bible-believing Christians as humble, because we are not. We are too focused on ourselves and too pleased with our own accomplishments. *Sexual immorality.* This is what had happened in Corinth (see 5 v 1-2). Again, this will stop Christ being glorified, and tear a church apart.

7. Read Genesis 2 v 18-25. In 1 Cor 11 v 8-10, Paul is looking back to the story of creation. Why is it helpful to be reminded of how things were in the Garden of Eden, before sin entered the world? Because we are seeing what God's plan was: how things were before the world became imperfect. Genesis 2 provides us with the pattern for how God wants husbands and wives to treat each other.

• **Why is the man the head of a marriage (1 Cor 11 v 8-9)?** Because of the order of creation: Eve was created from Adam. Woman was made for man, not man for woman. (Many questions may crop up here—look together at the rest of Q7, Q8 and Explore More, and then see if those questions have been answered.)

• **Why did God make woman (Genesis 2 v 18)?** Because without her, the man was "alone". He needed woman. And she is made to be her husband's "helper"; to support him as he leads her.
Many take this teaching as denigrating to women. While it can be abused this way, the task of helping is a wonderful reflection of the character and glory of God. We understand and believe in a trinitarian God—Father, Son and Holy Spirit. The Son is a faithful Son, who always does the Father's will, yet this in no way denigrates Him or His dignity, nor limits His person or His character.

⊗

• **God gives man the authority to name the animals (v 19-20). How does this shape our understanding of verse 23?** A sign of the man's loving authority in marriage is seen in Genesis 2 v 23, where

he names the woman. Naming someone is a sign of authority; so God gives man authority over creation (1 v 28), and then the task of naming the animals (2 v 19-20).

• **Does the man's authority in this marriage have an adverse effect on their relationship?** Not at all—in fact, quite the reverse! In v 23, the man is celebrating his wife, and how intimately interdependent they are—it is a (slightly strange!) love song. This couple were perfectly happy together (v 25, unlike every other married couple since).
We must beware the lie that a husband with authority over his wife is a husband who does not love his wife—in fact, sacrificial leadership of a marriage is a loving, unselfish thing for a husband to do. And after all, God is a God of authority as our Creator, yet is also perfectly loving toward His people (see 1 John 4 v 10).

EXPLORE MORE
Read Eph 5 v 22-33. Whose example of headship is a husband to follow (v 23)? Christ's, in the way He treats His people, the church.
What does this mean a husband will do for his wife (v 25)? He will be prepared to give himself up for her, "just as Christ … gave himself up for" His people. He did this by having their interests at heart in everything He did, supremely in giving His own life for them. A husband is to die to his own desires and comfort each day in order to do whatever is best for his wife—even being willing to die for her if this is what is required.
Why will it be a positive thing for a wife to submit to this kind of husband, do you think? Because she can follow his lead, knowing that he is seeking her good

in all he does. She can trust him to have her best interests—her growth in faith and godliness—at heart.

8. What does Paul tell us about men and women, particularly husbands and wives, in 1 Cor 11 v 11-12? God is author of all—both men and women are made in God's image (1 v 26-27), to know Him as their loving ruler; they are equally valuable. Men and women need each other, and are to depend on each other, bearing one another's burdens, particularly in marriage. Husbands need wives who will support and help them to be the men and the leaders that God is calling them to be, in the home and in the church. Wives need husbands who will lead them thoughtfully, prayerfully and sacrificially. Churches need the various abilities and approaches that God has given to men and to women. We need each other.

9. APPLY: If you followed your culture's values and beliefs, what would that mean for your: • church? Again, this depends on your culture. Since cultures swing back and forth in their emphases, over-stressing either hierarchical authority or egalitarian mutuality, it's likely that *either:*
- your church will be dominated by men, who seek to exploit women, refusing to allow them to have a voice, or to think of how the church can best serve their needs, while expecting and demanding that they serve them as men *or:*
- your church will allow women to have any role that a man has, exalting "equality" over biblical teaching, which reserves some authority roles in churches to men (see 1 Corinthians 14 v 34 and 1 Timothy 2 v 12). Men will therefore not be encouraged and challenged to assume the leadership roles God calls them to; women will be strongly encouraged, or even coerced, to assume

roles of leadership. And both men and women who seek to hold to the Bible's teaching will be branded intolerant and sexist.

- **marriages?** *Either:*
  - marriages will be places where women are treated no better than slaves. Husbands abuse their authority to seek their own comfort and pleasure, rather than using it to serve their wives *or:*
  - wives will not submit to their husbands, follow his decisions, or be loyal and supportive when he seeks to change something or direct the marriage in a particular way. And/or husbands will refuse to serve their wife by taking responsibility for the direction and health of the marriage, for the big decisions that life confronts marriages with, for the tone and approach for the raising of children, etc.

10. APPLY: If you allowed the Bible's teaching here to shape your values and beliefs, how would that change your:
- **church?** Essentially, you would avoid the answers to Q9! Men who have leadership roles will lead in a way which serves both women and men who are in the church membership—which sacrifices their own interests for others, which points away from themselves and towards Christ, and which always remains under the authority of Christ and the teaching of His apostles (see Q11). Women will not seek to point to themselves, nor to assume authority which God has designed men to have. They will work hard and serve well as equal members of the family of God.

- **marriages?** Husbands will lead sacrificially and prayerfully, putting their wife's faith and godliness before their own comfort, reputation or ease. They will take responsibility for the decisions and direction of the marriage. And wives will support and encourage their husband in this, enjoying being married to a man who serves with loving authority.

11. APPLY: Why is it easier for us to follow the culture of our day than the Bible? Because it means we won't be unpopular. We won't be called names we'd rather not be. More subtly, we can convince ourselves that if our churches are to grow, we need to copy our culture.

- **Why is it easier to follow the culture of a previous generation?** It is possible to mistake the way our church "has always done things" (ie: for the last fifty years!) with the way the Bible tells us our church should be. Some churches are good at resisting the influence of today's culture where it is unbiblical—but they can end up simply seeking to reflect the culture of the recent past, so that church becomes

a refuge from "the world outside". In many ways, this is easier than engaging with the culture—working out how our church can be welcoming to and engaging for newcomers without giving up biblical standards.

12. APPLY: Read 1 Corinthians 1 v 1. Why is it better for us to hold to the teachings Paul has "passed … on to" the church (11 v 2)? Because his teaching is apostolic. His words are not simply his own, but they are what God has appointed and inspired him to write. They may not prove popular or culturally acceptable (they do not seem to have been so in Corinth, so it should be no surprise when they are not today)—but they are God's teachings, for His people, passed down to us in His word. Holding to the teaching of 1 Corinthians 11 will mean we are living as God designed us to, under His authority, enjoying the blessing of life in God's world living God's way (see Psalm 1).

4 1 Corinthians 11 v 17-34
THOUGHTFUL UNITY

THE BIG IDEA:
The Lord's Supper reminds us of Christ's death in our place and our unity as a church. It challenges us to be thoughtful and loving towards our fellow church members, being united as Christians and serious about sin.

SUMMARY
Paul begins this section harshly—there is nothing to praise in the aspect of church life he is now focusing on. In fact what these Corinthian Christians are doing means their

meetings, the point of which is to build up and edify individual Christians and the church, are actually harmful (v 17).

What was so terrible? The Corinthians were divided, and these divisions were seen in the way they approached the Lord's Supper. Instead of being a celebration of sacrificial love, their suppers had become a time of selfishness. It seems that wealthier members of the church were able to arrive at the evening meetings earlier, and would eat the food and get drunk, leaving nothing for those poorer members who came later. This meal that stood at the center of the church's life as a symbol of Christian unity had become the indicator of how un-Christian, thoughtless and selfish they were.

Paul deals with this serious issue by reminding them what the Lord's Supper really is. It is a remembrance of Christ's atoning, sacrificial death (v 24-25); a renewal and recommitment to the covenant with God that He established (v 25); a proclamation of Christ's death as the center of church life (v 26); a reminder that Christ will return in glory (v 26). So it declares what unites a church—Christ Himself (10 v 16-17).

If we understand what the Lord's Supper is, we will do two things: first, we will seek to be united, and to show sacrificial love towards one another, just as Jesus has done to each of us. And second, we will treat sharing in this meal seriously. We will understand that coming to the table as a thoughtless, casual sinner brings judgment, not an assurance of forgiveness. So we will examine ourselves, recognizing and repenting of our sin, particularly that which causes division (v 28).

The Apply questions aim to move your group from Corinth to their particular church in the 21st-century. We may not be in a position to begin eating a fellowship meal before others arrive; but there are many things that we can thoughtlessly do which will cause or underline division within our membership. And we may not abuse the Lord's Supper in the same way as in Corinth; but churches today can do so in different ways, treating it flippantly and without due reverence; approaching it without time to self-examine, confess sin and be reconciled to anyone we're divided from; or simply by individual Christians not making a priority of attending.

GUIDANCE TO QUESTIONS

1. What is the point of the Lord's Supper, or Communion? How might we get the way we celebrate it wrong? Encourage one-sentence summaries! People may focus on mistakes in theology, or in attitude, or in church practice, though of course all are linked.

2. Imagine Paul was writing to your church about your Sunday meetings. How would you feel about his words in v 17 and v 20? Their very meetings were becoming harmful—when the whole purpose of having them was to build up and edify each member and to build up the church. Paul was also blunt about the meal they shared. Whatever they were doing, it was certainly not celebrating the Lord's Supper! If these words were addressed from an apostle to our church, we would (or should) be shocked, and concerned, and take his criticisms seriously.

3. What is happening in this church? Whose interests come first? The wealthy could arrive before those who were working. Apparently they were sharing a meal together, others joining as they arrived, with those who arrived last—those who worked ie: the poorest members—perhaps finding nothing left from the fellowship meal, and the wealthier members drunk. The poorer Christians were being left out. Perhaps this was not a deliberate policy—but it was the thoughtless consequence of people putting their own interests first.

- **Read 1 Cor 10 v 17. How were the Corinthians undermining the purpose of the Lord's Supper?** The meal that was intended to state that the church is one body, a fellowship united by faith in Christ and His death, was in fact a way in which some members were being left out.

4. Imagine that the Corinthian church, particularly the wealthier members, had been acting in exactly the opposite way to what they were. What would that church meeting have been like?
You might like to read v 33-34 at this point. People would satisfy their hunger at home, thinking carefully about how to serve and help others in the congregation. They would wait for everyone to arrive before beginning, would share the wine, and rather than enjoying the best for themselves, would give the best to those who in everyday life would not enjoy such good food. They would consciously be careful not to do anything that made the less wealthy feel belittled or excluded.

5. What contradictions between what we say we believe and how we actually live can go unchallenged today? These are very hard to spot! You might like to think of one that applies to yourself (as opposed to others) to get a discussion started.
Two broad beliefs which we might contradict in ways that will vary according to our culture and church contexts are:
• God is holy and pure, and we want to become like His Son; but then often we live in unrepentant sin in an area of our lives.
• We know Scripture is inspired by God, is flawless, and is the way He reveals Who He is to His people; but then often we fail to read, remember, or work to apply it.

6. How might your church membership thoughtlessly cause divisions between richer and poorer Christians:
• **as a whole church body?** Church trips or events which not everyone can afford.

This can perhaps be overcome by offering discounts or free places—but arguably, it is still divisive.
Expecting all members to have a large home library of Christian literature; or to have had a college education; or to be able to afford the latest technology.
Publicizing who gives what to the church.

• **as individuals?** Inviting church family members to our house for dinner and serving them expensive food, which they cannot hope to give us when we are invited back.
Talking about a new car, or new clothes, or a foreign holiday, with those who cannot afford such a lifestyle.
Wearing clothing which points out our greater wealth.
Talking about how we wish we could have a nicer kitchen/car/house to those who have less than us anyway.

7. When we share the Lord's Supper, what do we: • remember?
(1) Christ's substitutionary, atoning death, and the forgiveness of our sins won at the cross. The Lord's Supper moves us to meditate on the cost Christ bore in our place, on God's loving provision of a Savior. (2) The covenant, or relational agreement, Jesus established through His death. In the Old Testament, covenants were ratified by blood (see Hebrews 9 v 21-22); and God had promised a new covenant (Jeremiah 31 v 31). In taking the wrath we deserve and giving us redemption, Christ's blood starts the new covenant between us and His Father. As we celebrate the Supper, we pledge to God, and each other, and to the world that we are participating in this covenant.

• **underline as the message of Christianity?** "The Lord's death" (v 26).

It is, when we think about it, a strange message to have at the heart of our church and our lives, but it is, and must remain, the center of the faith we believe and proclaim.

• **look forward to?** The day when the Lord "comes" (v 26). We are not sharing a funeral meal; it is a dress rehearsal for the wedding supper of Jesus the Lamb. One day His people will sit and eat and drink with Him, physically (Luke 22 v 29-30).

8. How will sharing this meal and thinking of these things enable a church to stay united—rich and poor, old and young, mature and new believer? The Lord's Supper, when properly celebrated, humbles us, reminding us that we are all sinners, and all need Jesus' death in our place to be forgiven. We are all equal at the Lord's table.

It unites us, reminding us that Christ's death is the beginning and center of what makes us Christian believers. It declares that, whatever else makes us different from each other, we have the most important thing in common—faith in Christ and His death. It inspires us to love one another. By the Lord's Supper, we celebrate His sacrificial love—and we should give ourselves to reflect that kind of love to one another. If we know Christ has given Himself for us, we will give ourselves for our brothers and sisters. Christian love is real and practical, just as Christ's was.

EXPLORE MORE
Read Psalm 75 v 8 and Isaiah 51 v 17. What "cup" is to be drunk, and by whom? The cup of God's wrath, His deserved anger, is to be drunk by the wicked—by people who have rebelled against Him. That is, everyone.

Read Matt 26 v 39-42. What cup did Jesus drink, so that we might not have to? That cup of God's wrath. Notice how horrific the prospect of bearing God's anger was to the Lord Jesus.

Why does Christ need to drink that bitter cup in order to offer us the cup of new and eternal relationship, or "covenant", with God? Because we, as sinners, deserve to drink the cup of God's wrath. It is only because Christ drank it for others—for us—that He can offer us the cup that represents the new covenant of righteousness and eternal life with God.

Why is it right that the Lord's Supper is observed in every church? Because it is such an eloquent and telling testimony to Christ's death and its benefits. It points to the center of Christian belief and fellowship. And because the Lord Himself commands us to (1 Corinthians 11 v 24-25).

9. If we contribute to thoughtless division in the church, what does that bring (1 Cor 11 v 28-29, 31)? God's judgment, because it is sin.

• **How does v 29 help us to understand what Paul means by "an unworthy manner" (v 27)?** Verse 29 says we should not take this meal if we do not recognize and claim for ourselves the fruits of Jesus' death. If you partake of this meal without recognizing Jesus' life-giving rule in your life, you are eating and drinking judgment on yourself. You are seeing visually in the bread and wine that sin leads to judgment and death, but you are not asking Jesus to take that judgment for you—you are still under judgment.

This does not mean that we should only come to the Lord's Supper when we are sinlessly perfect. But we should not come if we are not serious about our sin—serious about recognizing where we have sinned, serious about accepting that sin deserves judgment, and serious about not continuing to live in a way which contradicts our faith.

10. How should Christians prepare for sharing the Lord's Supper (v 28)?
Q9 shows us why we want to examine ourselves before we take Communion. Christians should reflect on their life. To spot any contradictions between what we are celebrating in the Lord's Supper—humble unity in our Christ-won salvation—and the way we live. To repent of our sins and trust in the death of Christ. To make sure we are not coming to the table of the "one loaf" while divided in some way from a fellow Christian.

11. Why is it good that God disciplines His people when they sin thoughtlessly (v 32)? Because there is a consequence that is worse than illness, or even than physical death: God's "condemnation". God was disciplining the Corinthian church, through illness (v 30), so that they would see their sin, take it seriously, and come to the Lord's table in repentance and faith in Christ's death. His discipline is part of His goodness to His people—His warning to us to change and come back to the cross before it is too late. It is better for God to allow our lives to be difficult now, so that we come back to trusting Christ and don't wander away from Him, than never to know difficulty now, but turn away from Christ and face God's judgment beyond death.

12. In what ways could churches today undermine the importance and the message of the Lord's Supper, without meaning to do so? Some churches have explicitly changed the message of the Lord's Supper, eg: a church which teaches that the Lord's Supper is a re-sacrifice of the actual body and blood of Jesus, rather than a remembrance of His one-time sacrifice at the cross. But this question is focusing on unconscious undermining of the Lord's Supper. Two examples are: racing through the Lord's Supper at the end of a service, without proper time for preparation of reflection; allowing absolutely anyone to take the bread and wine, without making clear this is meal only for Christians who have "examined" themselves.

13. What should we think about during a Lord's Supper meeting?
• About Jesus' death, in our place, bearing God's wrath for our sins.
• About our membership of His covenant people, and our unity with the rest of our church.
• About the day when Jesus will return in glory, and we will sit and eat and drink with Him.

It may be that one of these things will particularly strike and move us during a particular time of sharing the Lord's Supper. **How might we feel?** What we think about will affect how we feel:
• Humbled, by the truth that the Lord had to die because of our sin. Perhaps even mournful.
• Grateful, for the Lord's death.
• Encouraged, as we see our Christian family around us.
• Determined, to live for the Christ who died for us, and to encourage others to do the same.
• Excited, as we consider being in glory with Him.

One thing we surely cannot be is unmoved!

5

1 Corinthians 12 v 1-31a

YOUR GIFTS, THEIR GOOD

THE BIG IDEA

The Holy Spirit has given God's people different gifts to use to build up Christ's body, the church.

SUMMARY

The Corinthian church had written to Paul about "spiritual gifts" (v 1). Some church members were using some of these gifts to point to themselves, and exalting particular gifts (especially speaking in ecstatic languages, or "tongues") over others, and so being divisive.

Paul stresses that Christians are united by having the same Lord, whose Spirit has worked in each of them to bring them under His rule and give them new life (v 1-3). This same Spirit is a gift-giving Spirit (v 4-7, 11), and He gives these gifts to Christian brothers and sisters to use to build each other up (v 7b)—for the common good. This is one major biblical reason for going to church—to exercise our gifts (which can be abilities or talents, but also simply the circumstances we are currently in) for the good of our church.

Paul introduces the image of the church as the body of Christ, an image he was introduced to by the risen Christ, when Jesus asked Paul as he travelled to Damascus to arrest Christians: "Why do you persecute me?" (Acts 9 v 4). Paul tells the Corinthians we are all part of one body, with one Spirit.

This has three major implications for us:

1. We are not to think of ourselves as useless church members, with nothing to contribute. God has arranged us into His body (v 18), and given us gifts to use (v 7, 11) for the body.

2. We are not to envy others' gifts, wishing we had different ones. We need to trust God in the way He has arranged the parts. We should think of how the church would be harmed if we all had only the gift we tend to envy others having! We are different, and deliberately so.

3. We are not to be proud of our own gifts, thinking of ourselves as better than others. As an eye needs to remember it needs a hand (v 21), so Christians need to remember that each part of the body is necessary, and no one part is more needed than another.

Uselessness, envy and pride all deny God's role in giving these gifts, as if we knew better than God how He should arrange the body of Christ!

Q10 addresses the question of speaking in ecstatic tongues (which is also looked at in the next session). The order in which Paul lists some of the spiritual gifts, in v 28-30, suggests that speaking in tongues is not the primary sign of faith, or spiritual maturity, nor a more important gifts than others. The sign of a Spirit-filled Christian is that they say: "Jesus is Lord" (v 3); the sign of a Spirit-filled church is that they use their gifts for each other (v 7), and share joy and suffering alongside one another (v 26).

GUIDANCE TO QUESTIONS

1. Why do people go to church? In a sense, the whole of 1 Corinthians is about how we ought to view church. Some people go to church for wrong reasons regarding salvation—the view that I am right with God if I go to church regularly (or a few times a year). But encourage your group to see that someone could be a Christian (know we are right with God through faith in Christ and His death for us) but also have basically self-centered reasons for going to church, eg:

- It's fun.
- It helps me with my faith.
- I see my friends there.
- It helps me be a better person/husband/wife/father/daughter.
- I get a lot out of the sermons.

Notice that these are not wrong ways to view church. But, as we'll see, Paul wants us to go to church each Sunday to build up the rest of the church, to edify our Christian brothers and sisters (as Q11 will pick up on).

2. How is it that anyone can stop worshipping "mute idols" (v 2) and accept Jesus as Lord (v 3)? Through the Holy Spirit. He is the source of the new life we find by taking Jesus as Lord of our life. It is only God's Spirit working in someone's heart that enables them to stop loving and serving things which cannot deliver, in this life or in our death, and realize who Jesus is, what He has done, and that we can and must say: "He is my Lord".

3. What else does the Spirit do for believers (v 4, 7, 11)?

- v 4: Gives us differing gifts.
- v 7: These are one of the ways we see the work of the Spirit in us—they are the outward "manifestation" of the inward work of the Spirit.
- v 11: He gives to each just what He wants.
- **Why had these "manifestations" been given (v 7b)?** For the "common good". We are to use our Spirit-given gifts to do good for our church. They are not given primarily for our enjoyment (though serving others does bless us too; see John 13 v 17); they are given to us so that we

might serve and help other believers in our church family. You might like to read 1 Peter 4 v 10.

4. What kinds of gifts does the Spirit give to God's people (v 8-10)? The list of gifts we find here is not meant to be a complete list of the "*charismata*", the gifts of God's grace to us. There are many things in the New Testament called "*charismata*", including God's gift of eternal life (Romans 6 v 23) and marriage/singleness (1 Corinthians 7 v 7). In 12 v 27-30, and in Romans 12 v 6-8, Paul repeats some of the gifts in v 8-10; he also adds some others. Don't get bogged down in exactly what each gift means—I am not sure Paul means absolutely distinct things by each one. "Prophecy" seems to have a wide range of meanings in the New Testament—here we might interpret it as basically the Spirit-inspired teaching of God's word to others, including both longer, prepared statements and shorter, spontaneous comments.

Note: The gift of speaking in tongues is dealt with in more detail in Q10.

5. APPLY: How is the Bible's view of our gifts different from what the world says about our abilities:

- **in where they come from?** The world says our gifts come from ourselves (our efforts or our genes). The Bible says they come from God, given through His Spirit.
- **in their purpose?** The world says we have our gifts to enjoy for ourselves. If we are good at something, it's our right to enjoy it, however we like. The Bible says that we are given our abilities, talents and circumstances in order to serve God's people and bring glory to God.

6. APPLY: How will remembering the

truths of these verses prevent us from using our gifts divisively or selfishly? We are united to the same Lord, Jesus (v 1-3), through the work of the same Spirit, who is the One who gives all our different gifts (v 4). We are united by the same Spirit, who dwells in each of us. Our gifts should not divide us, but unite us, if they are exercised as God intends (v 7b).

And God intends us to use our gifts not for our own strengthening, but for the strengthening of our church—not for our own ends, but in service of our church.

7. What image does Paul use here for the church (v 12-13, 27)? A body. We are all part of one body, with one Spirit—the body of Christ.

⊻

- Why do you think Paul chose to use the image of a body to describe the church?

8. How would verses 14-20 stop some Corinthian church members feeling useless as part of the church? The body is made up of many parts (v 14), and every Christian in the Corinthian church is part of that body, whatever their character, gifts, or role within that body. They are not the same as all the other members of the church, but they are no less important. A foot isn't excluded from a part of the body simply because it's not a hand (v 14)!

- **How would this stop them envying the gifts of others in the church?** By enabling them to realize their mutual dependence on each other. They need to trust God in the way He has arranged the parts (v 18)—God's Spirit has given them different gifts, and to envy someone else's gift is to think that they know better than

God. Instead of wishing they had someone else's gifts and not acting as part of the body because they don't, each Corinthian Christian needs to get on with living as the part of the body God has made them.

9. How would verses 21-26 stop some Corinthian Christians feeling proud of their role and gifts within the church? Again, by challenging them to realize their mutual dependence on each other. Pride in their own role means they are ignoring the importance of the different role of all the other church members. A body needs a head and feet (v 21)—a church member needs all the other church members. If a Christian has great gifts, they need—instead of being proud—to use them to honor those who are "weaker" (v 22-24).

⊻

- **How would understanding this have changed the attitude and actions of the wealthier Christians in the Corinthian church when it came to celebrating the Lord's Supper, which we looked at in the last session?** They would have used all the gifts the Spirit had blessed them with, including the circumstance of having wealth, to honor and serve those "we [ie: naturally, from the world's point of view] think are less honorable" (v 23), ensuring that "there should be no division in the body" (v 25). They would have waited for their poorer brothers and sisters, making sure they had the best of the meal, not the worst.

10. It seems the Corinthian church had decided that speaking in ecstatic, non-earthly languages—"tongues"—was a special gift, given to special Christians. What does the order of the gifts

mentioned suggest that Paul thought of that view? Tongues are last in the list, not first! Paul, under the inspiration of the Holy Spirit, understands the gift of tongues to be something from God, but they are no more special or exalted or spiritual than the gift of healing, or teaching, or administration. The order would suggest they are perhaps even not as notable as those gifts, with verse 31 underlining that they are not, in fact, the "greater gifts". As we will see in the next session, what is more important than any spiritual gifting is love. We should pray that God's spirit will work among us in whatever way He might desire; and His work will, verse 7, be geared toward the edification of the church as a whole.

We do not see the Corinthian practice of speaking in ecstatic tongues as part of the weekly public service talked about elsewhere in the New Testament. There are occasions in Acts of people speaking in tongues upon their initial conversion, but those tongues were ones that others could understand.

- **What is the real sign of being a Spirit-filled church (v 26)?** Rejoicing at each other's happiness, and endeavoring with tenderness and sympathy to bear each other's burdens and sorrows. Whereas in Corinth, one worshipped pagan gods simply by making individual sacrificial offerings and turning up to enjoy the great public feasts, Paul's instructions demand a context of committed relationships, where church members are bound together as one body, sorrowing and rejoicing together, so that the ups and downs of one member's life are treated as the ups and downs of every member's life.

11. APPLY: What has this part of 1 Cor taught us about why we should go to church? To build up the rest of the church,

to edify our Christian brothers and sisters. To use our gifts to serve the rest of our church membership; and to share the joys and sorrows of every other member of the body of Christ.

This means being at church weekly, recognizing that we have a responsibility to each other, and are mutually dependent on each other. If we are not at our church meetings every week, we cannot play our part in the body God has arranged us to be part of.

12. APPLY: How would you use this passage to respond to the following ideas: Encourage your group to point to particular verses in 12 v 1-31a as they respond.

- **"I love playing the piano in my jazz band, but I don't have time to play it in church as well. And anyway, I don't much like playing the type of songs my pastor chooses!"** This fails to recognize that this ability is Spirit-given (v 4, 11), and that He has given this gift to be used for the "common good" of the church (v 7b), not simply to be enjoyed as the one with the gift sees fit. So the ability of piano-playing should be offered to the church first and foremost—and then, of course, enjoyed if there is time and opportunity! Moreover, a Christian will increasingly find that the most blessed way to use their abilities is in the service of Christ and His people.

- **"I don't do much at church. There's nothing for me to do, really."** This person needs to be encouraged, and perhaps challenged, to see that every Christian is given a role to play in the body (v 14-15). They won't be gifted in the same way as others in their church—but God's Spirit has gifted them (v 4-6) to work for the body they are part of (v 18). They need to think: *There is a way I can work for the rest of the body. What is it? How can I serve?*

- **"I do a lot for my church. And to be honest, I wish everyone else was a bit more like me. Then we'd really get somewhere!"** This person needs to be challenged in two ways: first, to realize they depend on the rest of the body, and need to be served by the various types of gifts God has given to others and not to them. It is God's role to give gifts and arrange His church, not theirs! Second, to see serving using their God-given gifts as a privilege and humble responsibility, not as

a matter of pride.

- **"Real Christians speak in tongues."** The work of the Spirit in someone is to enable them to stop saying (in some way, perhaps very politely!): "Jesus be cursed" and begin to say: "Jesus is Lord" (v 3). That is the mark of someone who is restored in their relationship with God by the death of His Son and the work of His Spirit—and it will be seen in them as they use their God-given gifts to serve His people (v 7) and as they commit to identifying with God's people (v 26). This is the mark of a real Christian, not whether or not they speak in tongues.

6 1 Corinthians 12 v 31b – 14 v 40
THE MOST EXCELLENT WAY

THE BIG IDEA:

Love should guide the way we view our church, and the way we use our gifts for our church. We need love more than we need anything else.

SUMMARY

Note: Taken together, these two chapters are long, and at times difficult. I have kept them together in one study to show that the application for chapter 13 is mainly in chapter 14. But you may want to split it into two sessions for your group—in which case, a good place to split the study is just before Q7, after the Getting Personal section.

Chapter 13 is one of the most famous passages in the Bible. It is often used at weddings—although it is in fact a rebuke intended to be a guard against selfishness in how we view church.

Love is an absolute necessity, says Paul; without it, all our spiritual gifts and everything else we may be or do are nothing (13 v 1-3). And he also points out that love lasts (v 8-13). Our imperfect prophecy and knowledge are only partial and will eventually pass away as we come into the presence of God, where we will see and know Him perfectly. But God is love—to be with Him is to know and taste and experience perfect love—and so love outlasts all else, even faith and hope.

Paul says that loving use of our gifts is "the most excellent way" (12 v 31b)—so we should "follow the way of love and eagerly desire spiritual gifts" (14 v 1)—especially prophecy. Loving the church means edifying the church, and Paul points out that this happens through prophecy rather than through uninterpreted tongues, which seem to have been so beloved of and exalted by this church. The church is built up by Spirit-led utterances of truth in languages we can understand (v 3-4).

Paul finishes by pointing the Corinthian church to his apostolic authority. If anyone really is "spiritually gifted", they will recognize and submit to Paul's authority, because he brings them "the Lord's command" (v 37). This is the sign of real spiritual maturity—not speaking in tongues or anything else.

Note: There are three difficult and controversial issues in this passage which may well be mentioned by your group as they work through. Paul often mentions prophecy. We do not exactly know what these prophecies were. It is unlikely they were foretellings of the future. Generally, they seem to have been anything from preaching to simply talking together about gospel truth in conversations. We have no reason to think that the Spirit has stopped leading us in this way.

Paul also writes that women should "remain silent" (14 v 34). This appears to be in the context of public evaluation of prophecies (a discussion of which precedes it in chapter 14). It is clear from chapter 11 that this is not an absolute command to silence, since Paul speaks without disapproval of women praying and prophesying in church meetings. But they should not have been yelling out questions—such questions should be directed to their husbands outside the assembly.

Speaking in tongues is the final controversial issue. Q10 helps your group think carefully about how neither to over-exalt speaking in tongues, nor to make too little of this spiritual gift. Many churches tend towards one error or the other.

GUIDANCE TO QUESTIONS

1. What makes a really good church member? There are many partially right answers to this, and many answers can be offered. Paul in chapter 13 is going to say that an attitude of love is the most important thing (12 v 31b). If someone comes up with "love" as the answer (possibly because they have read the passage already!), ask why this is the case.

2. Pick a couple [of the aspects of love listed in v 4-7] that strike you. What would each of these aspects of love look like in everyday life? Encourage your group to come up with short, realistic real-life scenarios for the qualities you choose. To cover more of them, you could divide up Paul's list of what love is, and isn't, between pairs in your group, and then ask them to come up with real-life outworkings of those particular qualities and report back to the group. But don't spend a whole study on this question!

3. How impressive-looking is the Christian Paul is describing in verses 1-3? In one sense, very! They speak in tongues (v 1); they prophesy—they have great insights into and knowledge of God's word (v 2); they engage in social action and are prepared for martyrdom (v 3). A Christian like this in your church would be amazing! But... Paul says all these things are "nothing" without love. The Christian being described is nothing, if they are not loving (v 1). Love is absolutely necessary, Paul says.

• **This is the kind of believer the Corinthians wanted to be, or saw themselves as. How would these verses shock them?** Because they could have all the things they aspire to in the Christian life, and yet without the love that Paul defines in verses 4-7, they are "nothing". It is better to be a loving Christian than a hugely gifted Christian, or a preaching, knowledgeable, generous, self-denying Christian.

4. What contrasts does [Paul] draw between our experience as God's people now, and our experience as God's people then? Maturity will replace childishness (v 11). Prophecy and knowledge will pass away, but love will remain, even in the celestial atmosphere of the unmediated presence of God. When sight and knowledge are perfected, and our senses are filled full with God's perfect glory, then we will see that love is even greater than faith and hope (v 13). We will have what we have hoped for, and we will have been given what we trusted Jesus to give us. Heaven will be all about love. We will love God, and each other, perfectly, rather than in part, because we will see Him face to face (v 12).

- **How is this exciting?** Because it is what we were made for—to love and be loved by God, to know Him completely. All our current joys and love for God are just reflections of what we will one day enjoy. **How is it humbling?** Because it reminds us that we are mere children in our knowledge and appreciation of God. We may know more than others, but we don't know anything like what the saints in heaven know.

EXPLORE MORE
Read 1 John 4 v 7-21. What do these verses tell us about:
- **what love is?** Love is what God shows us (v 7); it is who God is, as the Trinity loves each of the other persons in the Trinity (v 16); it is opposed to fear (v 18).
- **where love is most clearly seen?** Verse

10—at the cross, where God's Son died as an "atoning sacrifice". That is, He gave His life to make atonement for our sins—to pay the punishment for them, and so to make us "at-one" again with His Father.
- **what difference love makes to us?** We love each other with the kind of love God showed us in Jesus (v 11-12). We experience God's love and God's presence as we love others (v 16). And we don't have fear, because we have confidence that God in His love has done everything necessary to bring us through the day of judgment (v 17-18).

… Look back through Paul's definition of love in 1 Cor 13 v 4-7. How do we see each of these love-inspired qualities as we look at the Lord Jesus? How much time you spend on this question will depend on how well your group know the Gospel accounts of Jesus' life. There are, of course, many examples the Lord Jesus showing each of these qualities, and many of them are seen most clearly in His loving death on the cross. The hardest is perhaps "envy", where you might like to mention how the Son never seeks to usurp His Father's position, but joyfully submits to and obeys Him (eg: John 6 v 38; 14 v 28-31).

5. APPLY: How is 1 Corinthians 13 a wonderful passage to use for:
- **confession?** It shows us where we are not living lives of love, and prompts us to seek forgiveness for the ways in which we do not love others as Christ has loved us.
- **thanksgiving?** Who personified this love better than the Lord Jesus?! How can we not praise the Son for how He has loved us, as we read this wonderful list?
- **prayer?** We will be driven to ask God to change the quantity and quality of our love, as we read here about real love.

• **reconciliation?** When two parties are divided, it is because of a failure of love on one side or the other, or both. These verses encourage us to focus on ourselves, to see where we are not loving the other in the way Christ loves us. If both parties decide to love each other in a 1 Corinthians-way, reconciliation, though not easy and often painful, becomes possible.

6. APPLY: Read John 13 v 34-35. What does a loving church do? Reflects Jesus' love for us. Jesus said this is how the world around us knows that we are His disciples. So this kind of love is vital to our evangelistic task.

• **Do people see something different in your church because of your love for each other? How? How not?** Make sure you don't talk about how you see your own church, but how the community around your church sees it, or how a non-Christian visitor experience it. How would they see you loving one another? Encourage your group to come up with practical examples, both of how you do love each other in the sight of nonbelievers around you, and how you could do this more.

7. Why is prophecy [Spirit-led utterances of biblical truth] better than speaking in tongues in church?
• **[1 Cor 14] v 2-11?** Prophecies strengthen, encourage and comfort others (v 3), but speaking in tongues only helps the speaker (v 4). Prophecy is intelligible, and edifying the church requires understanding (v 9).

• **v 13-17?** Prophecy, which everyone can understand, engages both heart (or "spirit") and mind. It enables others to agree, and to praise God by saying

"amen" to the truths about Him someone has just said.
• **v 23-25?** Even unbelievers are better served by intelligible speech than by words that are unintelligible. Unbelievers will think Christians are crazy if they come to a church where everyone is speaking in tongues (v 23). Prophecy, on the other hand, as it praises God and shares the gospel of Christ, is used to convict and convert.

If you're going to work through the Explore More below, look at one (or all) of these questions for after that.
• How could you make your meetings, and what you say in them, more intelligible to unbelievers?
• How could your church make the offense of the gospel clearer?
• Does your church need be more obviously exclusive?

EXPLORE MORE
Re-read v 20-22. … What would be the sign that judgment had come (v 21)? Unknown tongues. Hearing foreigners talking was the sign that foreign invasion had happened—that God's judgment had come on the unbelieving Israelites.
So, when a non-Christian visits a church, what does the "sign" of speaking in an unintelligible tongue point to? It's a sign of God's judgment on believers (v 22). Tongues produce (are "for") unbelievers, who know they are not part of the people of God as they sit in a church and fail to understand what is going on.
But what kind of people does prophecy produce? Believers (v 22, 24-25). Prophecy will share the gospel of Christ in a way people can understand. It will offer salvation

through faith to the nonbeliever, and will point to the glory of God. As people hear the gospel, and watch Christians praising God in ways they can understand, some will realize that the church is the community of God, where He dwells, and will worship Him (v 25).

8. How should the character of God (v 33) be seen in His people's gatherings: Paul says the meeting should reflect God's character, and He "is not a God of disorder, but of peace" (v 33).

• **v 26?** Everything that occurs in our meetings should be done for the purpose of strengthening the church. That means we will be unselfish with whether and how we use our gifts.

• **v 27-28?** Tongue speakers should be limited in the meeting. They should not dominate the whole time the church is gathered—and if there is no interpreter (who can tell others what the tongue-speaker is saying, so that all might participate and be built up), then tongues should not be spoken at all.

• **v 29-33?** Those prophesying should be kept under the authority of the church (which sits under the authority of Scripture). So everything someone says, in preaching or applying or bringing a word from the Lord, should be "weigh[ed] carefully" against what we know God has said in His word (v 29). Prophesy should not become rivalry—people should speak one after another (v 30-31). Prophets should exercise self-control (v 32).

• **v 34-35? (Note: 11 v 5 indicates that this silence is not absolute. It probably relates to shouting out during services to ask questions.)** Women should not interrupt the meeting to yell out questions to their husbands! If they have a question,

it should be directed to their husband, or another elder or teacher, outside the meeting itself.

9. What does Paul say a truly mature Christian will do (v 36-40)?

• Recognise that Paul's teaching is from God (v 36-37), and sit under Paul's authority as an apostle, rather than ignoring it (v 38).

• Be eager to prophesy—ie: to proclaim God's truths in a way which is intelligible, encouraging and edifying.

• Not rule out speaking in tongues altogether.

• Ensure that they use their gifts in an orderly way. Passion and order should go together in our meetings, to communicate the truth about God.

10. APPLY: How do these chapters help us:

• **not make too *much* of speaking in tongues (or any other particular gift)?**

• 12 v 27-31a: Speaking in tongues is not a greater gift than any other, and it is not something that every Christian will have the ability to do (the sign that someone is a believer, filled by the Spirit, is that they say: "Jesus is Lord", v 3).

• 13 v 1: It is more important to have love than to be able to speak in tongues. An unloving tongue-speaker is just a noisy cymbal!

• 14 v 1: It's better to prophesy than speak in a tongue.

• 14 v 18-19: Five words of understandable Bible teaching are better than 10,000 words spoken in an ecstatic language.

• 14 v 22-25: Tongues do not encourage unbelievers to look into the gospel; nor are they the way in which they come to recognize and worship God.

- **not make too little of speaking in tongues?**
  - 12 v 30; 14 v 18: Speaking in tongues is a spiritual gift, for which those who have it can thank God.
  - 14 v 26-27: There is nothing inherently disorderly or undesirable about speaking in a tongue, as long as it is done in an orderly way, and is interpreted so the rest of the church can understand it.
  - 14 v 39: No church should forbid speaking in tongues.
  Speaking in tongues is a controversial issue in many churches, denominations and networks. There is nothing inherently undesirable about using this spiritual gift in a church meeting. If we desire to give a message in tongues, we should seek out our pastor to talk about it.

- Are there ways in which your church makes too much, or too little, of certain gifts? Which? And how? How can you help your church grow in maturity in these areas?

11. APPLY: What is the most excellent way to be a good church member?
To make our priority loving our church as Christ loves us. This will mean gathering on Sundays to praise God and encourage each other; we'll be eager to use our spiritual gifts in a way which reflects God's character of order, and which edifies the church, and not in a way which points to ourselves or is only for our benefit. We'll see building up the church as our job, as well as everyone else's.

7 1 Corinthians 15
RESURRECTION: HOLD ON

THE BIG IDEA
The resurrection of Jesus Christ is a fundamental part of the true gospel, and the basis of our hope for the future and our lives now. We must hold firmly to it!

SUMMARY
This chapter is all about the resurrection of Christ from the dead—why it is fundamental.

Paul says three things:
- The resurrection is an essential part of the Christian message (v 1-11). The Corinthians' continued adherence to the gospel is essential to their salvation (v 1-2), and the resurrection is part of that gospel

message (v 4). Undermining or denying the bodily resurrection of the Lord Jesus is to change and lose the true gospel.

- The resurrection is an essential part of the Christian life (v 12-34). If Christ has not been raised (v 14, 17), the consequences are terrible. "But Christ has indeed been raised from the dead" (v 20)—and this is our great hope. The good news is that salvation does exist, and this guarantees our future resurrection (v 21-23), and the future destruction of all opposition to God, when Christ's rule culminates in the reign of God over everything (v 27-28).

- The resurrection will be bodily, real, and glorious (v 35-58). In the resurrection we will have a body—a body similar to our bodies in this life, but also very different—spiritual, powerful, glorious, imperishable. Paul points to the risen Christ as the example of a resurrected body—we will be like Him, with bodies like His (v 49).

And so Paul urges the Corinthians to stand firm in believing in the resurrection of Christ, and their own future resurrection (v 58)—and to see that doctrine and life go together, and so, with their future secured, they must give themselves to the work of the Lord in the present.

GUIDANCE TO QUESTIONS

1. What will life after death be like? Let people share their views, whether or not they come from the pages of the Bible. It may flag up some areas of misunderstanding among your group (for instance, that it will involve having a soul but not a body).

• **If we stopped 100 people in the local supermarket and asked them this question, what additional answers would we get?**

2. What are the essential aspects of the gospel message?
• Christ (v 3) (easy to miss this one!): God's promised all-powerful, restoring King is the central subject of the gospel.
• died for our sins (v 3): His death was on behalf of ("for") us, in our place.
• He was buried (v 4): He was truly dead.
• He was raised (v 4): We know Christ died for our sins because He was raised.
• He appeared (v 5-6): Paul writes of the eyewitnesses who confirm the truth of the resurrection. We can be confident He was truly raised to life because He was seen, by different groups at different times.

• According to the Scriptures (v 2, 4): The Old Testament predicted Christ's crucifixion and resurrection. He lived and died and rose in fulfilment of their prophecies.

• **Why can we be confident that Christ "was raised"?** Because it was predicted in the Old Testament (eg: Isaiah 53 v 1-12; Psalm 16). And because the risen Jesus appeared to so many different people. At the time the Corinthians read this letter, there were at least 251 people (v 6), plus apostles, still alive who could have backed up Paul's claim that Jesus had risen.

3. How do the Corinthians need to relate to this gospel message, and why (v 2)? They need to "hold firmly" to it. If they do this, they are "saved". But Paul warns them that if they stop trusting it, their previous belief will be "in vain", useless. Ongoing trust in the gospel of Christ is what saves us.

4. APPLY: How do people and even churches today alter the various parts of the true, apostolic gospel message? Work through the aspects of the gospel message (Q2), thinking about how these truths are undermined. Some suggestions:
• *Christ.* Jesus is often re-made into a gentle, meek and mild Jesus who is a friend but not a King—who does not much mind how we live our lives, and who is not angry with our rejection of Him. (See Psalm 2).
• *Died for our sins and was buried.* Muslims teach that Christ did not really die. On the other hand, many churches teach a false gospel which ignores the reality of our sin, and/or the judgment of God on it. This leads to a misunderstanding of why Christ died. The cross becomes merely a

tragedy; an injustice; an example of love; a sign that God understands our pain. It is all those things, but supremely it is the place where God Himself bore our sins so that we might be forgiven.

- *Was raised and appeared.* This is normally a dividing line between Christians and non-Christians. (For a good resource on the historicity of the resurrection, read The Case for Christ by Lee Strobel.) Sadly, many churches also suggest that Jesus did not really rise physically: that this was only a spiritual reality, or is a metaphor.

- *According to the Scriptures.* The Old Testament is often (wrongly!) treated as something that Christ replaced, rather than fulfilled; or even as a series of books which present us with a different God to the one Jesus came to reveal.

- **Why do even small changes matter?** The gospel is where we discover how God has come to the world Himself in Christ, to die in our place and rise to life so that we can have eternal life. If we change the gospel, we change what we believe in; and we are no longer believing in the real Jesus, who alone can save.
How should we respond? We need to respond to "small" changes by insisting on "holding firmly" (v 2) to Paul's gospel, which was identical to the gospel of the other apostles (v 11). We need lovingly but firmly to oppose any attempts to change, whether from good motives or bad, the true gospel—not only for our own sakes, but for the sakes of others who are in danger of letting go of the message which saves.

5. Why does this matter (v 13-18, v 29-32)? If Christ Jesus has not been raised from the dead…

- Paul's preaching is for nothing (v 14).

- our faith is useless (v 14).
- the apostles are liars (v 15-16).
- there is no assurance of divine forgiveness—so faith is futile, useless (v 17)
- believers who have already died are lost, rather than enjoying eternal life (v 18)
- some of the Corinthians' own practices are contradictory, such as "baptizing for the dead" (v 29).
  Note: We are not sure exactly what Paul is referring to here. Paul may be saying: "Why baptize someone who is going to perish for eternity? What's the point?" (This is how early church preachers, such as Tertullian and Chrysostom, understood his words here.) Whatever he meant exactly, Paul's point is that the very practices of the Corinthians themselves were inconsistent with there being no resurrection.
- Paul putting himself in danger (v 32— "wild animals" might be his description of facing a riot in Ephesus, see Acts 19 v 23-41) was pointless.

- **If there is no resurrection, what are Christians (v 19)?** The most pitiable people in the world. We have spent our lives for a lie, for nonexistent salvation.

- **If there is no resurrection, why is the saying Paul quotes at the end of verse 32 the sensible way to live?** If death is the end of everything, then this life is all there is. So we might as well get on with enjoying ourselves as best we can today ("eat and drink")—because death mocks all the gifts we have and give. We will be nothing beyond death, so we should focus on ourselves and on what feels good in the here and now.

6. Work back through those verses and pick out why the fact of Jesus' resurrection is such good news. Get your

group to turn each part of their answer to Q5 around to complete the sentence: "Since Christ HAS BEEN raised…"

- Paul's preaching is worthwhile.
- so is faith in the gospel message he preaches.
- the apostles are trustworthy truth-tellers.
- we have assurance that we are forgiven— our faith in Jesus' death for our sins is sensible and necessary.
- believers who have died are with God in glory.
- (since "baptism for the dead" is both unclear and never commanded or even commended in Scripture, you might skip this!)
- it is worth Paul putting himself in danger to reach people with the gospel message.
- point people to verse 19, too: we are in a better, not worse, position than all other men—because through faith in the crucified, risen Christ, we have forgiveness of sins and eternal life.

7. What does the resurrection guarantee about the future:

- **for Christians (v 23)?** When Jesus returns, believers will be raised to eternal life in just the same way that He was. He is the "firstfruits" of resurrected eternal life—the first instalment, the guarantee it will happen for His people one day.

- **for everything (v 24-28)?** What a splendid, majestic picture Paul paints! Christ will destroy all opposition to God. His reign, which began at His resurrection, will continue until it culminates in the destruction of death—the ultimate enemy of God's purposes—and then God will reign in all creation. The victorious Son of God will ultimately subject Himself to the Father. The order of this universe will be restored.

8. APPLY: How should the reality of the resurrection change our lives? A

good way to think this through is to look at how it changed Paul's life. The resurrection should mean that living for eternity will be our perspective, with living with Christ as King, and sharing His gospel message as our priority. No sacrifice for Christ or His gospel will be too great. There will be nothing in this life that we will have to have, or count as more precious than what is still to come—because we will know where we are headed.

- **Why is it tempting to live as though the end of verse 32 were ultimate reality?**
  - We are surrounded by people who have this attitude towards life and death, and so it is easy to be carried along by them.
  - We cannot yet see how glorious our resurrected life will be, but we can see the things of this world—we find it hard to live by faith, and not by sight (2 Corinthians 5 v 7).

9. How will our resurrection "spiritual" bodies be different from our "natural" bodies now?

- **v 42-44:** Our present body is: perishable (it will not last); one of "dishonor" (we use it to sin, and so it does not reflect God as it should); one of "weakness" (it breaks); "natural" (ie: it is part of this natural world, of which death and decay is a part). Our resurrection body is: imperishable (eternal); one of "glory" (perfectly in God's image); one of "power" (it will not break); "spiritual" (ie: having eternal life, part of the future world, where nothing dies or decays).

- **v 50-54:** Our future body will not be flesh and blood like now (v 50). This isn't to say it won't be a real, physical body—Jesus' risen body was real (see, for example, Luke 24 v 36-43). But it will be changed (v 52) in the sense that it will no longer be mortal flesh and blood which does not last, but immortal (v 53). Our bodies will no longer be subject to death (v 54).

10. How does our sin make death painful—something that stings (v 56)?
Sin leaves us facing God's judgment and wrath beyond our death. Death feels unnatural and wrong, and according to the gospel, death *is* wrong—it was not part of God's original creation, and it is the result of sin. But it is eternal, spiritual death of sinners' separation from God that is the real "sting" of physical death.

- **How does the gospel message (v 3-8) show us that death now has no sting for Christians?** Christ's resurrection proves our sins have been dealt with by Him in His death; it guarantees that we will be raised; and it shows us what our resurrection life will be like. Death is not a sting anymore: suffering will give way to glory, and our frustrations and pains here will give way to fulfilment, satisfaction and joy for evermore in the presence of God.

EXPLORE MORE
Read Gen 2 v 7 and Dan 7 v 13. Where does the first man, Adam, come from? The dust of the earth. And, once he has sinned, he will return to dust (Gen 3 v 19). **How about the "son of man" in Daniel's God-given vision?** He came from heaven. **What does being "in Adam", or like Adam, mean for us (1 Cor 15 v 21-22, 48-49)?** Death came through Adam—so "all die" (v 21-22). By nature, we are like him, bearing his likeness (v 48-49). Paul is probably thinking both that our bodies are like his—made from dust, destined to

return to dust—and that our hearts are like his—sinful, rejecting God's rule.
Why is it wonderful to be "in Christ", made like Him through faith in Him (v 21-22, 48-49)? Because in Christ, people are "made alive" (v 22), because resurrection from our "in-Adam-death" comes through Him (v 21). And, amazingly, Christ's people will "bear the likeness of the man from heaven". We will enjoy a body like Christ's resurrection body, and a character like Christ's. In eternity, we will be like Christ.

11. APPLY: As Christians, how should we view death?
We do not need to fear death, or to grieve for Christians who die as though they are lost. Death is something we go through on the way to Christ's new creation, where we will enjoy perfect resurrection life in glorious, immortal bodies. Our best days are assuredly ahead of us.

12. APPLY: What does Paul want us to do between now and our deaths (v 58)?
Stand firm (in believing in the gospel message—see verse 2), not letting anything stop us placing our faith in the crucified and risen Lord Jesus. And get on with giving everything we have to living God's way. Standing firm in the doctrine of the resurrection will change how we live. We will not live for ourselves, and for the moment; we'll live for the future, and be willing to give up anything in order to work for the God whose presence we will enjoy being in beyond death.

13. APPLY: Why is the resurrection important?
This is a great way to sum up the study:
- It is the great proof that God accepted Christ's death in our place, for our sins.
- It proves the apostles' teaching (ie: the New Testament) is trustworthy—they

suffered and even died for the truth of the resurrection.

- It means our faith in forgiveness of sins is correct.
- It guarantees our resurrection, and shows the kind of bodies we will have: immortal, glorious, undecaying.
- It means death has no sting, because it is just something that lies between our lives here and our lives in eternity.
- It changes the way we live now, meaning we can give ourselves fully to working for God as we look forward to the future He will give us, rather than feeling we must live for ourselves in the present.

8 1 Corinthians 16
GOOD EXAMPLES

THE BIG IDEA

We serve our church by remembering we are part of God's people worldwide and following examples of Christians who show a strong love for Jesus and His people.

SUMMARY

Paul writes 1 Corinthians to reshape the thinking of the believers in Corinth so that they will redefine the church, not along lines of self-expression and individual interests but along lines of humble, self-denying love and care. This is how their struggling, deeply flawed church can be turned around.
And those are the underlying themes of this last chapter of the letter.

In encouraging them to give to Christians they have never met, and by sending greetings from the church in a different province, Paul encourages the Corinthian church to have a larger vision: to know that they are part of something much larger than their local congregation.

In sending greetings and setting out his arrangements, Paul also gives this church positive examples to follow. There is, of course, himself: but there is also Timothy, a worker for the Lord (v 10-11); Stephanas,

Fortunatus and Achaicus, who are "devoted" to fellow Christians and refresh the spirits of other believers; and there are Aquila and Priscilla, who had lived in Corinth when the church was planted (Acts 18), and who serve the church in Ephesus by opening their house for it to meet there.

All this revolves around verses 13-14 and verses 22-24—which return to a great theme of the letter, a call to robust love. The Corinthian church was under attack, from false doctrines, division, compromise and immorality. They needed to learn to love, and to learn what love does—it stands guard, stands firm, defends truth, perseveres courageously. This love must be for Christ's people (v 13-14) but most of all for Christ Himself (v 22).

Paul finishes by talking to this messed-up church of his "love to all of you" (v 24). He loves these people enough to confront them with uncomfortable challenges; to teach them rather than ordering them; to work hard instead of simply giving up on them.

It was out of Christian loving strength that he wrote this letter. We will be greatly helped by using it diagnostically with our own congregations in view, hearing Paul's encouragements and challenges for our lives as a local church.

GUIDANCE TO QUESTIONS

1. How do people suggest struggling churches can be turned around? This is a huge question, and could take up your whole time together! Some possibilities (though you may come up with others):

- By altering its service times/orders/ language/structures (eg: break into lots of smaller groups)
- New leadership
- Come up with a mission statement
- Inject some finance (possibly by having a giving campaign)
- Pray
- Ask another church to send some keen, well-taught members
- Teach the gospel more clearly.
- Teach the gospel less clearly.
- They can't—let them die gently.

Few churches presented more challenges than the Corinthian one, and Paul does not appear to be giving up on it. It's worth returning to this question at the end of the study, as a way to recap Paul's teaching in chapter 16, and the whole of 1 Corinthians.

2. What have been the main points of Paul's teaching in this letter to a struggling church? For the first half of the letter, the study headings in the first Good Book Guide on 1 Corinthians, *Challenging Church*, will help. For chs 10 – 16, you could use the "Story So Far" summaries at the beginning of each study.

3. What does Paul say about how this local church should relate to churches elsewhere?

- v 1-4: There was a great famine engulfing the people, including the church, of Jerusalem. Paul encouraged churches from his missionary journeys to collect money to send to those Christians many miles away who were in need. The local church in Corinth should give its money wisely and generously to Christians who are in need—even if, as in this case, they had never met them and were unlikely to, and as Gentiles had nothing ethnically or culturally in common with the Jewish Christians in Israel.

- v 19-20: Paul shows them a larger vision of love and care that stretches between congregations. By sending these greetings from congregations around Ephesus, across the Aegean Sea, Paul is reminding this local church that they are part of something much larger. They can learn from other congregations (see 11 v 16; 14 v 33); they can give to them (16 v 1-2); they can encourage and pray for one another.

EXPLORE MORE

Read 2 Cor 8 v 7-15; 9 v 7-11. What further guidelines about Christian financial giving are given here?
It is something to strive for excellence in (8 v 7); should be proportionate to our wealth (v 12-13); given voluntarily and joyfully (9 v 7).

Why do Christians give up their own comfort to give money to others (8 v 9; 9 v 8)?
8 v 9: Because Jesus gave up far more, and experienced far worse, in order to give us the riches of heaven. Our giving reflects our appreciation of His.
9 v 8: because we trust that God will give us what we need, so we don't need to have the security of money in the bank.

Why do many Christians find it hard to see their finances as Paul does, do you think? Because the world doesn't! And because it involves relying on God, not ourselves.

4. What do we see in 1 Cor 16 about Paul's own priorities? Paul cares enough about churches to visit them as well as write to them (v 5). And he is willing to spend time working in and for this congregation, despite (and because of) the challenges (v 6). His priority is the church; and preaching the gospel which brings people into the church. There seems to have been an evangelistic opportunity in Ephesus (v 8-9), a time of special blessing and growth for that church, and he wanted to make full use of it. That's why he won't come to Corinth immediately. Notice that Paul's priority is to do the Lord's work, even when it involves facing opposition (v 9). His priority was never an easy life!

Note: Though v 13-14 help answer this question, these verses are the subject of Q7 and 8, and best left till then.

5. Who does Paul mention as examples of Christlike living? What do you think he wants the Corinthian Christians to learn from each of them?

Timothy (v 10): "He is carrying on the work of the Lord", and that is what counts. It seems that the Corinthians would rather see Paul or Apollos than Timothy, but Paul exhorts them to provide for Timothy. They should love teachers who teach the gospel, whether young or old, weak or strong, the one they wanted or not.

Stephanas, Fortunatus and Achaicus (v 15-18): They gave themselves to serving God's people (v 15), and sought to encourage churches and church leaders (v 18). To a church which seemed to have become self-seeking and uncaring of each other, these men were examples of preferring to do what others need than what they want; who gave themselves in caring for others; who inconvenienced themselves with great regularity for God's people.

Aquila and Priscilla (v 19): For more on this couple, see Acts 18. They had become models by their service of hosting the church. Churches didn't have buildings set aside for their meetings; someone had to go to the trouble of hosting the congregation. Again, the Corinthians can learn from such selfless service. They have been meeting to serve themselves (11 v 17-22); this couple have been giving up their home to serve their church.

6. APPLY: If the people mentioned in this passage were members of your church today, what would they be doing and saying? Think of specific actions the attitudes of these people towards their church would inspire in your setting and church family.

• **How would they be challenging you?** This is an opportunity for your group to think about what these people would do differently to what people today naturally do, and how they naturally view, church. Encourage the group not simply to identify how these people would be different, but to think about how they each could become more like them.

7. How does v 13 help us understand what it looks like to obey Paul's command in v 14? To "do everything in love" (v 14) does not mean to be weak, to be accepting of all things, to give in rather than risk causing offence. It means being alert to dangers to the health of our church; insisting on teaching and living out the true gospel; and opposing anything or anyone who would seek to undermine our brothers and sisters in doing that. It means having the courage to stand up for what is right, however unpopular that may make us. Christian love is a strong love. We need this combination of verses 13 and 14, just as both Paul and Christ Himself had.

- **Think of the problems this church was struggling with. How would obeying Paul's words here turn the church around?**
  - "Be on your guard": against allowing sin to go unchecked; against selfishness; against idolatry and legalism
  - "Stand firm in the faith": against teachers who don't preach and live out the cross; against denial of core doctrines such as the resurrection
  - "Be men of courage": rather than accepting division, stand up for unity; don't be swayed by being popular and "wise" in the eyes of the surrounding culture.
  - "Be strong. Do everything in love": look out for other Christians before your own interests; give up your freedoms whenever they might obscure the gospel message; use your gifts for the church, not your glory.

Of course, there is overlap between Paul's commands here and the areas this church needed turning around.

8. How does v 22 help us understand what it looks like to obey v 14?
Supremely, we must love Jesus Christ. God has made us and deserves our wholehearted affections. And His Son has died for us to redeem us and so doubly deserves our love. The start and end of the Christian life is loving the Lord Jesus. If we don't, we are not part of God's people.

9. Verse 22 is a warning. Why is verse 23 such good news for flawed churches and flawed Christians (that is, you and me)? We see our failures within the church.

Unbelievers see them too. We do not love Christ as we should. But we can go forward as believers, and as a church, because "the grace of the Lord Jesus [is] with you". Grace is favor and blessing given despite us. It means we can be forgiven through the death of Christ on the cross;. It means a church, however flawed, can be used by God and bring God glory, as long as it seeks to love and submit to the Lord Jesus.

10. Why is verse 24 an astonishing way for Paul to finish his letter? You might like to read 1 v 1-9. We should marvel that Paul begins and ends with such kind comments when everything in between has shown us what a messed-up church this is. Paul has identified and challenged their foolish, worldly-minded divisions, their astounding tolerance of immorality, their gospel-denying litigiousness, their confusion over marriage, their selfishness, and their resurrection-denying heresy—and then in closing he says: "My love to all of you in Christ Jesus"! **What does it tell us about Paul?** Paul loved people. He loved the body of Christ. He could have responded in anger over the years it seemed he had wasted in Corinth, the prayers expended to no apparent purpose, the teaching he'd given that had been ignored. Instead, he communicated in loving concern. His love meant he was prepared to challenge this church, sometimes (as we've seen) sharply. His love meant he was willing to take time to write, and to visit. Paul's letter epitomizes the strong love of verses 13-14.

11. APPLY: What are the areas covered in 1 Corinthians which your church most needs to hear? Again, you might like to read the contents of this Good Book Guide and the one on 1 Corinthians 1 – 9 (see Q2). Remind them of how the letter contains

encouragements as well as challenges! Your church may need to hear a "keep going" message rather than (or as well as) a "turn around" message.

Give people a minute or so to think about their individual answer to this question, and then share. Encourage people not to be complacent in their answers ("I think we're doing fine, really") but equally not to be too critical.

• **How could you help your church to become more like Paul's goal for the Corinthian church?** Talk about what you could do as a group and/or individuals. Be specific rather than general.

PRAY

This is a slightly shorter study than the previous ones, in order to allow you more time to pray at the end, since you've come to the end of 1 Corinthians.

IX 9Marks   Is your church healthy?

9Marks wants to help churches grow in these nine marks of health:

1. Expositional Preaching

2. Biblical Theology

3. A Biblical Understanding of the Gospel

4. A Biblical Understanding of Conversion

5. A Biblical Understanding of Evangelism

6. Biblical Church Membership

7. Biblical Church Discipline

8. Biblical Discipleship

9. Biblical Church Leadership

Find all our titles and other resources at www.9Marks.org.
9Marks exists to equip church leaders with a biblical vision and practical resources
for displaying God's glory to the nations through healthy churches.

Also available in the Good Book Guide series...

OLD TESTAMENT

NEW! Esther: Royal rescue
7 studies. ISBN: 9781908317926

1 Kings 1-11: The rise and fall of King Solomon 8 studies.
ISBN: 9781907377976

Ezekiel: The God of Glory
6 studies. ISBN: 9781904889274

Jonah: The depths of Grace
6 studies. ISBN: 9781907377433

NEW! Hosea: God's love song
8 studies. ISBN: 9781905564255

NEW TESTAMENT

Mark 1-8: The Coming King
10 studies. ISBN: 9781904889281

Mark 9-16: The Servant King
7 studies. ISBN: 9781904889519

Romans 1-5: God and You
6 studies. ISBN: 9781904889618

1 Corinthians 1-9: Challenging Church 7 studies.
ISBN: 9781908317691(US)/...506 (UK)

1 Thessalonians: Living to please God 7 studies. ISBN: 9781904889533

1 Peter: Living in the real world
5 studies. ISBN: 9781904889496

1 John: How to be sure
7 studies. ISBN: 9781904889953

Revelation 2-3: A message from Jesus to the church today
7 studies. ISBN: 9781905564682

TOPICAL

Promises Kept *Bible overview*
9 studies. ISBN: 9781908317933

Biblical Womanhood 10 studies.
ISBN: 9781907377532

Biblical Manhood 10 studies.
ISBN: 9781904889977

Experiencing God 6 studies.
ISBN: 9781906334437

Women of Faith from the OT
8 studies. ISBN: 978190488952

Women of Faith from the NT
8 studies. ISBN: 9781905564460

The Holy Spirit 8 studies.
ISBN: 9781905564217

Contentment 6 studies.
ISBN: 9781905564668

Visit your friendly neighborhood website to see the full range, and to download samples
N America: www.thegoodbook.com • UK & Europe: www.thegoodbook.co.uk
Australia: www.thegoodbook.com.au • New Zealand: www.thegoodbook.co.nz

thegoodbook
COMPANY

At The Good Book Company, we are dedicated to helping Christians and local churches grow. We believe that God's growth process always starts with hearing clearly what He has said to us through His timeless word—the Bible.

Ever since we opened our doors in 1991, we have been striving to produce resources that honour God in the way the Bible is used. We have grown to become an international provider of user-friendly resources to the Christian community, with believers of all backgrounds and denominations using our Bible studies, books, evangelistic resources, DVD-based courses and training events.

We want to equip ordinary Christians to live for Christ day by day, and churches to grow in their knowledge of God, their love for one another, and the effectiveness of their outreach.

Call us for a discussion of your needs or visit one of our local websites for more information on the resources and services we provide.

USA: www.thegoodbook.com
www.thegoodbook.co.uk
Australia: www.thegoodbook.com.au
New Zealand: www.thegoodbook.co.nz

N America: 866 244 2165
UK & Europe: 0333 123 0880
Australia: (02) 6100 4211
New Zealand (+64) 3 343 1990

www.christianityexplored.org

Our partner site is a great place for those exploring the
Christian faith, with a clear explanation of the gospel,
powerful testimonies and answers to difficult questions.

One life. What's it all about?